BORN AGAIN POLITICS
and the MORAL MAJORITY:
What Social Surveys Really Show

BORN AGAIN POLITICS
and the MORAL MAJORITY:
What Social Surveys Really Show

ANSON SHUPE and
WILLIAM A. STACEY

Studies in American Religion
Volume 5

The Edwin Mellen Press
New York and Toronto

Library of Congress Cataloging in Publication Data

Shupe, Anson D.
    Born again politics and the Moral Majority.

    (Studies in American religion ; v. 5)
    Bibliography: p.
    Includes index.
    1. Moral Majority, Inc. 2. Public Opinion--
United States. 3. United States--Moral conditions
--Public opinion. 4. United States--Religion--
1960-   . 5. Christianity and politics.
6. Social surveys--Texas--Fort Worth metropolitan
area. 7. Social surveys--Texas--Dallas metropolitan
area. I. Stacey, William A. II. Title. III. Series.
HN90.M6S54 1982   303.3'8   82-8078
ISBN 0-88946-919-9   AACR2
ISBN 0-88946-920-2 (pbk.)

    The Edwin Mellen Press
    P.O. Box 450
    Lewiston, New York   14092

Studies in American Religion   ISBN 0-88946-992-X

Printed in the United States of America

Dedicated to all the people who
participated in this study.

PREFACE

This study was not funded by any government agency, denomination, or academic institution. We believe that is an important fact to establish for readers at the outset of this report in light of the intense controversy its findings have generated. When we released initial results from the 1981 Dallas-Fort Worth Metroplex Survey Project on grass roots support for the Moral Majority to the public through the media, a number of contradictory, sometimes emotional reactions were immediately forthcoming. It is worth briefly reviewing these reactions in order to validate our reaffirmation of the study's basic integrity (i.e., its financial autonomy from any funding source).

First, our professional colleagues in sociology and religious studies gladly welcomed further information on the phenomenon variously known as the New Religious Right, the New Christian Right, and "Born Again Politics". Much of our data directly addressed for the first time what others had debated passionately in the absence of firm evidence. It was, after all, for them as a professional/scientific audience that we designed the study and interpreted its results.

Second, reporters in the mass media (both the press and the electronic media) displayed rather unabashed delight in discovering systematic evidence that confirmed what many of them had begun to suspect: namely that much of the claims of the New Religious Right and the electronic church's defenders to attract and sway large numbers of persons (particularly at the polls) was sheer "hype", more an expression of wishful thinking and Madison Avenue advertising tactics than reality. Some news commentators expressed skepticism at our findings; many others, however, concurred in private and shared their own reinforcing impressions. Indeed, as we shall show, national surveys independently conducted added only support for our findings. In any event, given the saturation of the airwaves and front pages of newspapers with news of politically active conservative Christian evangelists, the Dallas-Fort Worth study's findings became sensationalistic to an extent that may surprise future observers familiar with the (now emerging) general historical picture of the New Religious Right's limited support base.

Third, sympathizers with the New Religious Right movement and/or programming on the electronic church reacted to our findings with outrage, angrily confusing the message with the messengers. We were contacted at our offices and homes, accused of being atheists, godless humanists, and worse. We were assailed by long-winded letters covered with scribbled Bible-verses and pestered by annoying, haranguing telephone calls. Our University's administration was the object of community pressure, and more than once we were physically threatened. Indeed, one author was forced to change his telephone number after several weeks of continued harassment.

The point of the previous paragraphs is that the responses to our research reported here were varied and likely revealed much about both attackers/accusers and sympathizers. Moreover, those who did not agree with our findings invariably charged us with premeditated bias and malicious, anti-Christian hatred. As our data show, such criticisms were misplaced. A number of persons suspicious of what agency, group or person had funded such a study, and to those critics we reply (as we did initially): no one. The 1981 Dallas-Fort Worth study of grass roots support for the New Religious Right represents non-funded research. The interviewers were volunteer graduate and undergraduate stu-

dents and one work-study assistant.* The former students
included a few altruistic souls who had a personal curiosity
in the findings, students being trained in research metho-
dology, and several persons intending to use the data for
master's theses. All costs were covered out-of-pocket.
Contrary to the current image of large grants underwriting
most survey research, a good deal of social science survey
data is gathered on such an impecunious, *ad hoc* basis. That
it is necessary to reaffirm this fact to our critics who
suspect our motives is undoubtedly a good indicator of the
social threat, at least implicit, that some will feel in
any social science data.

Anson Shupe, Associate Director
William A. Stacey, Director

Center for Social Research
The University of Texas at Arlington

*We wish to thank in particular Jan Parker, JoAnn
Nawn, Susan Stacy, Ed Vaughn, and, certainly not least,
Kristy Smith for their efforts. This monograph represents
Reports Number 20 and 21 of the Center for Social Research.

TABLE OF CONTENTS

Chapter   I: The Question Of Popular Support
                 For The New Religious Right . . . . . .   (1) —

Chapter   II: The 1981 Dallas-Fort Worth Metro-
                 plex Survey Project   13

Chapter III: Empirical Perspectives On A New "Politi-
                 cal" Movement: The Moral Majority . . . (29) —

Chapter   IV: The Moral Majority: Religious Or
                 Political Movement?' . . . . (47) —

Chapter   V: The Moral Majority From the Minority
                 Vantage Point . . . .   65 ?

Chapter   VI: Perspectives Of The Clergy Toward
                 The Moral Majority. . . . .   (75) —

Chapter VII: A Critical View Of Popular Support
                 For The New Religious Right . . . . . .   93 —

Chapter VIII: What Shall We Make Of The Moral Ma-
                 jority And The New Religious Right. . . (103) —

Appendix   :   Additional Tables For Chapter Six . . . 107

Index   :   114

CHAPTER I

THE QUESTION OF POPULAR SUPPORT FOR
THE NEW RELIGIOUS RIGHT

The beginning of the 1980's witnessed a coterie of aggressive, well publicized evangelical Christian groups attempting to influence state and federal governments to adopt
conservative social policies on such issues as abortion, homosexuality, pornography, and national defense. Such organizations, which included the Lynchburg, Virginia-based Moral
Majority, Inc. of Reverend Jerry Falwell and the Religious
Roundtable inspired by Fort Worth, Texas evangelist Reverend
James Robison, worked hard during the 1980 presidential/con-
gressional elections alongside groups such as the National
Conservative Political Action Committee and the Conservative
Caucus to promote conservative candidates and defeat those
they defined as liberals. After the election, in which it
has been generally acknowledged that conservatives scored
impressive victories, both Falwell and Robison claimed to
have had an impact in mobilizing voters. Certainly candidate Ronald Reagan deliberately courted their support, as
seen at the Public Affairs Briefing conference hosted by the
Religious Roundtable in Dallas in August, 1980 when a large
number of evangelical Christian clergymen made their

1

conservative political views known to him. After the election as well, there were indications that President Ronald
Reagan felt some indebtedness to his evangelical supporters,
such as his publicized telephone call to Jerry Falwell in
1981 "to explain" his decision to nominate Judge Sandra
O' Connor to the Supreme Court (O' Connor possessed a past
state legislative/judicial record on abortion and the Equal
Rights Amendment anathema to conservatives) and his appoint-
ment of Robert Billings, former executive director of the
Moral Majority, Inc. to the White House staff as a liaison
to the religious community. But to what extent do outspoken
evangelical pastors involved in the New Religious Right (or,
as it is known by alternate euphemisms such as the New
Christian Right or Born Again Politics) actually represent
mainstream public sentiments? Can they legitimately claim
a united constituency in terms of consensus on specific social issues? Moreover, what is their potential for trans-
lating whatever sympathetic public sentiments they identify
with into significant political activity? These are the basic questions that motivated our study and guided its de-
sign.

THE RESURGENCE OF CONSERVATIVE CHRISTIANITY

Historian David Edwin Harrell, Jr. (1981:2) has re-
ferred to the famous 1920's Scopes "monkey trial" in Dayton,
Tennessee, with all the embarrassment and discredit it
brought to conservative Christians, as "the last hurrah of
pre-World War II fundamentalism". Anti-evolutionists became viewed not only by the press but also by the mainline
Christian public at large as eccentrics and atavistic fanat-
ics.

Conservatives' influence in many mainline denominations sharply declined. As Harrell noted, fundamentalists

in particular went underground as far as public notice was
concerned. However, they did not disappear.

> It was widely assumed for at least half a century
> that the Dayton debacle had killed almost all of
> them. . . . It was never so. The fundamentalists
> were still there -- up in the coves and the hal-
> lows, milking the cows, driving the trucks and trac-
> tors, in the cinder block churches that lined
> the railroad tracks. [H.L.] Mencken mused while
> riding the train back to Baltimore from Dayton
> that one could throw a brick out the window al-
> most anywhere in route and hit a fundamentalist
> on the head. But, they seemed remote and bizarre,
> and they talked funny, generally with a Southern
> drawl. Their leaders were increasingly eccentric
> and narrow -- Carl McIntire, Bob Jones, Sr.,
> John R. Rice; the flock was scattered into bickering
> sects (Harrell,1981:2).

It is not our purpose here to analyze the background
of the New Religious Right and its ties to the controversial much-publicized "electronic church." This has already
been done adequately by others. Thus we will not recount
the reemergence of conservative and fundamentalist Christianity as a "respectable" (i.e., non-sectarian) and widespread social movement in American culture and politics
since World War II, nor will we document its shift away
from political and social issue disengagement to a new,
aggressive stance of social concern. Harrell (1981,1975),
Quebedeaux (1980, 1976) and Kelley (1972) have examined
these trends elsewhere, as has Jorstad (1981) who traced
the "cultural maturation" of Born Again Christianity from
its low ebb in pre-World War II America through 1976 and
the election of Jimmy Carter to the White House during what
became known as the "Year of the Evangelical" to Ronald

Reagan's 1980 presidential victory. Nor have we the space
to examine the history of evangelicals' use of the "electronic church" (see Armstrong, 1979) and some of its members' involvement with the New Right political movement
(see Hadden and Swann, 1981).

It is sufficient to note that the current evangelical
"revival" did not emerge abruptly, that its roots are known
and explainable, and that it displays continuities with earlier conservative American Christian movements both in this
century and earlier. This country's religious history would
seem to suggest a cyclical pattern of Christian revivalism
and slump. If so, the current phase (for if there is such
a cyclical pattern, then we are indeed witnessing merely a
phase, perhaps the peak before the decline) illustrates
both the regularity of certain types of religious fervor in
our culture and the interesting possibilities for innova-
tion, such as employing technology not available during previous revivals, at each juncture.

INTIMATIONS OF WIDESPREAD POPULAR SUPPORT FOR
THE NEW RELIGIOUS RIGHT

As stated above, the basic but critical questions we
have asked of the New Religious Right are concerned with the
actual level of popular grass roots support of its specific
organizations and leaders, the consensus on certain social
issues within whatever subpopulation does support the movement, and (ultimately) the movement's potential for mobilizing sentiments of support into political activity. Without
anticipating our findings in the following chapters, there
were cogent reasons at the start of this study to expect a
large popular support base, particularly among the voting
home-owning middle class that Falwell is clearly seeking to
attract. But simultaneously we might also have logically

expected only a minority of committed but nevertheless a-
typical citizens in that support base. Let us briefly consider each alternative.

[Intimations for widespread support immediately suggest
themselves. Various evangelical leaders demanding new moral
leadership and a revitalization of American civil religion
have seemed able to mobilize large numbers of supporters.]
In April 1980, for example, the Washington for Jesus rally
staged at the nation's capitol -- billed as a non-partisan,
non-political positive event but in actuality a fairly
straightforward fundamentalist/evangelical Christian pro-
test against liberal social policies in the federal government -- drew approximately 200,000 participants from across
the United States. In September, 1981 at a Pro-Life Rally
in Dallas, Texas that included Jerry Falwell and James Robison as well as anti-Equal Rights Amendment spokesperson
Phyllis Schlafley and other New Right luminaries, a projected
attendance goal of 12,000 persons was not reached but approximately 4,000 people were present.

[Perhaps more important, secondary analysis of data
from a nationwide probability sample of Americans (Simpson, 1981) indicated that substantial (even majority) percentages of the population are in agreement with basic elements of the platform of the Moral Majority, Inc., the pre-
mier organization within the New Religious Right, on issues
of homosexuality, school prayer, women's roles in family and
society, and abortion. Meanwhile, the Moral Majority, Inc.
has claimed (quite correctly) to have established chapters
in most states.] It also claims to have registered three
million Christian voters (a less validated figure) and to
have raised $1,500,000 (Simpson, 1981:12). [In early 1980,
Jerry Falwell claimed that 25 million persons watch his syndicated "Old Time Gospel Hour" television program; shortly
before the Republican Convention's nominations of president

and vice-president, during an attempt to dissuade Ronald
Reagan from choosing George Bush as a running mate, Falwell
upped the figure to 50 million (Hadden and Swann, 1981:47).
While the accuracy of those latter figures may be questioned, there is no doubt that the number of people supporting Falwell's organization increased. For example, the Moral Majority's funds doubled in 1981 (*Dallas Times Herald,* 1981b).

Lastly, there is the election of Ronald Reagan to be
reckoned with, particularly since Reagan courted evangelical favor so heavily on the campaign trail, and the fact
that there is a strong, growing evangelical "mini-movement"
on Capitol Hill. For example, fairly large numbers of congressional persons regularly participate in evangelical
prayer breakfasts and prayer groups. Suplee (1981) commented:

> An estimated 800 of the 8,000 Senate staff are
> active in dozens of weekly evangelical gatherings.
> . . . Next year, when Congress takes up issues
> such as abortion, busing, school prayer and tu-
> ition tax credits for parochial schools, it will
> do so in a context of growing evangelical ac-
> tivity.

INTIMATIONS OF LACK OF POPULAR SUPPORT FOR
THE NEW RELIGIOUS RIGHT

Yet at the same time that we can find confirming indications of growing strength and popularity for the New Religious Right, there are signs that much of this "popularity" may be merely a product of media "hype," engineered by
slick public relations promotions and otherwise Madison Avenue tactics. In one study that reviewed media polls such
as a CBS poll taken of over 12,000 New York voters outside
election stations on election day, 1980 (Lipset and Raab,

1981), it was found that Democratic congressional candidates marked for evangelical/conservative attack did, on the whole, about as well (or as poorly) as non-targeted candidates. Interestingly some Republican candidates resented the style of "strong", unsolicited evangelical support they had received. Lipset and Raab (1981:30) concluded from their review:

> What all these findings seem to indicate is that the efforts to mobilize a religious constituency for political purposes in America had no measurable effect on the 1980 elections.

In a survey of Muncie, Indiana voters Johnson and Tamney (1981) also found an absence of evidence that conservative Christian groups had influenced support for Ronald Reagan's candidacy. Likewise, Hadden and Swann (1981:141) have argued that "the concept of New Right does not refer to the resurgence of conservative forces in the United States, but rather to a fairly small group whose common bond is mastery of the uses of modern communications technology." This technology includes, on one hand, the syndicated religious programming of the electronic church *and* the utilization of word processers, computers and cross-indexed mailing lists that, by creating pseudo-personal contact with larger numbers of viewers and listeners, allow "televangelists" like Oral Roberts, Pat Robertson and Jerry Falwell to tap an audience responsive to evangelical appeals for financial support. At the same time, however, despite its apparent small absolute size, Hadden and Swann did not dismiss the potential of such a fledgling movement for growth and expanding influence in politics, especially considering the sophisticated, well-financed technology supporting it and the driving sentiments undergirding its efforts:

The anger and moral indignation of these conservative groups run deep and their resent-
ment has been building for a long time. Perhaps what infuriates them most is the fact
that they don't believe the rest of society,
and the government in particular, has tak-
en them seriously. They are tired of being treated as a lunatic fringe or just
another interest group that isn't strong
enough to be factored into political decisions (p. 134).

Recently there has also been accumulating evidence to
suggest that the actual viewing and card-carrying audience
that would logically constitute the support base for media
pastors most active in the New Religious Right is considerably smaller than the evangelists' own claims both before and after the 1980 election. Sociologist William Martin (1981:11) cited Nielson rating figures of approximately
one million viewers and 400,000 viewers for Jerry Falwell
and James Robison, respectively. Hadden and Swann (1981:51)
reported slightly higher Arbitron rating figures for Falwell (1,455,720), but the picture of modest support similarly emerged. Likewise, Hadden and Swann (1981:65) sug-
gested that Falwell's subscription figures for the *Moral
Majority Report* newsletter in November, 1980 (a little over
one-half million) offered a better index of committed support for the Moral Majority, Inc. than Falwell's free-wheel-
ing estimates of tens of millions announced to Ronald Reagan
and others.

Such "corrective" bits of information began to accumu-
late throughout 1981. A Harris poll in July of that year
reported that a two-to-one majority of Americans felt that
it was improper for "Moral Majority Preachers" to put pressure on television networks and advertizers to remove

so-called "immoral" programs from the airwaves, even in the
Bible-belt South (Harris, 1981). One associated press re-
lease (reprinted in the *Dallas Times Herald,* 1981a) noted that
television's ten most viewed gospel programs had lost more
than 600,000 viewers between May, 1980 and May, 1981, not
an inconsiderable loss given the maximum audience size for
religious television that hovers somewhere around nine-to-
ten million viewers. Finally, *Newsweek* magazine reported in
late 1981 the following development that boded ill for Jerry
Falwell's future political influence:

> White House political analysts have concluded
> that an endorsement by the Rev. Jerry Falwell
> can amount to a kiss of death, and they want
> Republican candidates to avoid it if possible.
> "You don't want to lose their support," a
> Presidential aide says of Falwell and his
> Moral Majority, "but you don't want them
> out front and publicly with you." The ana-
> lysts are convinced that Falwell's elec-
> tion-eve endorsement of J. Marshall Cole-
> man helped Charles S. Robb beat the GOP can-
> didate in the recent Virginia gubernatorial
> race. According to surveys conducted by the
> Republican National Committee, Falwell is
> now unpopular among voters by margins of
> 2 to 1 and 3 to 1 all over the country, even
> in the Bible belt (*Newsweek,* 1981).

THE PURPOSE OF THIS STUDY

The portraits of the New Religious Right that emerge
are diametrically opposed: one of a growing, dynamic movement representing the "gut feelings" of most decent, tax-
paying, voting, and often ignored Americans and responding

to their sense of frustration over incompetent, morally a-
drift leadership; the other of a considerably narrower conservative Christian perspective that has long been pushed
out of the limelight and that now has the realistic hope,
through mastery of sophisticated technology, to make its
wishes and views disproportionately felt in America's high-
est political offices and power centers despite its minority
status. In other words, along with other Americans we are
faced with the conflicting reality claims of two partisan
groups: claims of a possibly aggrieved majority versus the
claims of possibly small groups of moral crusaders trying
to lend their religion the stamp of law.

Determining estimates of these segments of the larger
public, both ordinary citizens as well as clergymen, that
are in agreement with the social issue platforms of New Religious Right groups such as the Moral Majority *and* that
wish to see that platform translated into political legislation will do more than merely help settle the current debate over the real size of the New Religious Right's constituency. Such findings will also contribute toward a
better long-run understanding of American pluralistic society in which religion and politics exist in perennial tension and perhaps inform us about conditions under which
such tension periodically erupts noticeably beyond its usu-
al state. Furthermore, since much of the New Religious
Right -- in particular some of its most outspoken leadership -- is part of the emerging electronic church about
which few non-apologetic studies yet exist (see, e.g., Hadden and Swann, 1981 as opposed to Armstrong, 1979 and Bakker and Lamb, 1976), an examination of the impact of the
New Religious Right on the larger population will provide
some assessment of media religion's capacity to mobilize
political power as well as a measure of its popular support.
As Hadden and Swann (1981:201) concluded in their study

Prime Time Preachers,

How the electronic preachers utilize this enormous power base will have important implications for the future of this nation, indeed of our world.

In this study we take the preliminary but necessary step toward assessing this (potential) power base. We ask a set of interrelated questions to be dealt with in separate chapters:

(1) To what extent can we say that demographic measures such as age, income level, formal educational level, and occupation are related to support for the Moral Majority among the general citizenry?

(2) How is support for the Moral Majority related to conservative Christian beliefs (orthodoxy), media attendance (religiosity), church participation (religiosity), and civil religious sentiments?

(3) Given the claims of interdenominational support by outspoken Moral Majority leader Jerry Falwell, what is the real extent of such support across various religious denominations?

(4) Moreover, what is the level of ethnic support for the New Religious Right? Is it white, Anglo-Saxon Protestant (WASP) crusade or one to which other ethnic and racial groups subscribe?

(5) Finally, aside from ordinary citizens, how do *clergymen* perceive the New Religious Right? How many ministers and priests in a Bible-belt site such as the Dallas-Fort Worth Metroplex, where support should logically be maximized, really approve of New Religious Right groups such as Jerry Falwell's Moral Majority and James Robison's Religious Roundtable? How do they feel about the electronic church and how do they judge its impact? Is clerical support for the New Religious Right truly interdenominational

or does it follow along rather traditional (i.e., sectarian or denominational) lines?

These are questions whose answers will help more clearly define the dimensions, limits, and possibilities of the New Religious Right. No single study can definitively settle the controversial issues underlying them, but evidence gathered with their salience uppermost in mind may contribute to a better understanding of the 1980's most important socio-religious phenomenon.

CHAPTER II

THE 1981 DALLAS-FORT WORTH
METROPLEX SURVEY PROJECT

The 1981 Dallas-Fort Worth Metroplex Survey Project actually consisted of two related surveys aimed at sampling
two specific subpopulations: the general home-owning middle
class citizenry, and Christian clergy who pastor local congregations. Before discussing the details of each survey,
however, it is worth briefly emphasizing the importance of
this particular research site in order to later place our
findings in broader context.

THE DALLAS-FORT WORTH METROPLEX

The Dallas-Fort Worth Metropolitan Area (Metroplex) has
a population of almost four million people, making it as
large or larger than either Mississippi or Louisiana. It is
located in north-central Texas in the heart of the Bible-
belt (or, as one journalist acquaintance put it, in the
"buckle" of the Bible-belt). Within this urban area can be
found the Southern Baptist Convention headquarters (as well
as the nation's largest Southern Baptist congregation) in
Dallas and the James Robison Evangelistic Association as

13

well as the conservative Religious Roundtable (of which
Robison is a charter member) in nearby Fort Worth. The
Metroplex area hosted both the National Affairs Briefing at
which Ronald Reagan and other conservative politicans and
candidates appeared during the 1980 presidential campaign
and a major Pro-Life Rally in 1981. Both events were attended with great fanfare and media coverage by not only
Jerry Falwell and James Robison but also by nationally
prominent conservative political lobbyists such as Howard
Phillips and Paul Weyrich and anti-Equal Rights Amendment
advocate Phyllis Schafley.

In addition to the considerable publicity associated
with these and lesser events in the area, the Dallas-Fort
Worth Metroplex was saturated during the late 1970's and
early 1980's with daily media coverage of two related con-
troversies. The first was a local television station's re-
fusal to allow evangelist James Robison to purchase further
air time after he criticized homosexuals. Robison sued the
station, and an intense "Freedom of Speech/Freedom to
Preach" campaign ensued, as evidenced by newspaper adver-
tisements on Robison's behalf and pro-Robison billboards
and automobile bumper stickers.

The second topic concerned a series of sensational
court trials involving millionaire Cullen T. Davis (a Fort
Worth industrialist acquitted of charges of murdering his
step-daughter and shooting his estranged wife and of hiring
a "hit-man" to assassinate the judge presiding at Davis' di-
vorce trial) whom Robison was given credit for converting to
evangelical Christianity. Upon acquittals and remarriage
Davis and his new wife became staunch supporters (both theo-
logically and financially) of Robison, appearing often on
the latter's behalf on television talk shows, in media interviews, and regularly at local fundamentalist congregations. At such times the Davises testified to his and her

conversion experiences and condemned the alleged effects of
such phenomena as secular humanism and Darwinian evolutionary theory in public schools. Thus Davis' trials and
subsequent often discussed conversion further reinforced
the theology and social views of evangelist Robison for consumers of Dallas-Fort Worth media. Indeed, in 1981 it
would have been difficult to have been a regular television
news viewer or local newspaper reader and not have known
about Davis and his "born again" conversion.

Thus we maintain that because of denominational and
evangelistic activities within the Metroplex as well as other events mentioned, we have in this Bible-belt urban location a population to provide the "acid test" for uncovering
what support exists for the New Religious Right. As Hadden
and Swann (1981:156-157) noted in their review of Arbitron
television rating data, the New Religious Right, insofar as
it involves "television ministries," is largely a southern
phenomenon. Perhaps nowhere else in the United States has
any metropolitan area received as thorough a diet of media
coverage of precisely the topics with which the New Religious Right is concerned. Success or failure to uncover
substantial grass roots support for the New Religious Right
in this location should serve as a harbinger for what we
might expect in other southern (urban) areas and for anticipating the presumably lower support to be found in north-
ern and western states. In other words, though not gathered
nationally our findings from this area should have national
implications. Strong support for the Moral Majority discovered in the Dallas-Fort Worth Metroplex, of course, does
not necessarily mean that such support will appear in any
degree beyond the Bible-belt, but failure to find strong
support here would cast serious doubt on finding it in any
appreciable amounts anywhere else.

USE OF THE TERM "MORAL MAJORITY"

Throughout this analysis we will make frequent reference to the term "Moral Majority" as if it were synonymous
with the entire New Religious Right. The Moral Majority,
Inc. was founded in 1979 by Baptist minister Jerry Falwell
and is unquestionably the best known organization in the
New Religious Right movement. We maintain that Falwell's
outspoken support of presidential candidate Ronald Reagan
and later association with conservative political elites,
coupled with Falwell's growing electronic media presence,
have virtually turned the proper name "Moral Majority, Inc."
into the generic label "Moral Majority" that is understood
by the general public as equivalent with the New Religious
Right movement. Thus readers may assume (as we believe does
the public) that the term Moral Majority as used here represents not only Jerry Falwell's group but also the larger
conservative movement seeking to infuse politics with evangelical Christian morality.

THE 1981 DALLAS-FORT WORTH
GENERAL POPULATION SURVEY

Our initial interest in designing the spring, 1981
General Population Survey was to gather a large number of
supporters of the Moral Majority so as to be able to compare them with non-supporters. From studying the writings,
interviews, and sermons of Falwell, Robison and others, we
determined that our chances of maximizing the number of
Moral Majority supporters in our sample would be best
served by "going after" predominantly white, upper-middle/
middle-middle/lc.er-middle class homeowners (though as we
shall see in Chapter Six we did include some minorities

unavoidably in the survey). After inspecting the 1970 Census
(unfortunately comparable 1980 information on social class
and residential areas was not yet available), and mindful
of the fact that this region had experienced enormous in-
migration during the previous decade, we used local real-
tors as knowledgeable informants to update identification
of predominantly white home-owning upper-middle/middle-mid-
dle/lower-middle socio-economic areas in each of eight Metroplex municipalities. The eight municipalities sampled
were Arlington, Bedford, Dallas, DeSoto, Euless, Fort Worth,
Grand Prarie, Hurst, Irving, and Pleasant Grove. In each
municipality, in other words, we identified the three types
of middle class areas and then randomly selected neighborhoods within each in what amounted to a two-stage procedure.
Then teams of trained graduate and undergraduate students,
supervised by Center for Social Research staff at the University of Texas at Arlington, went into those selected
neighborhoods on weekends and in the evenings and distributed questionnaires containing 78 question-items to all
households where adult heads of households were at home.
Respondents were allowed to answer the questions in the pri-
vacy of their homes, our assistants collecting them after
approximately an hour's time.[1]

A total of 905 adult respondents were asked to participate in the survey. A total of 771, or 85 percent, re-
turned useable questionnaires.[2] Sixty respondents in the
sample were either black or Hispanic. In order to preserve
some degree of racial/ethnic homogeneity in the larger subsample, these minority respondents were deleted and analyzed
separately (see Chapter Six).

The remaining 711 respondents were then classified as
supporters of the Moral Majority, as indifferent (neutral)
toward the Moral Majority, or as non-supporters (negative)
of the Moral Majority. Supporters were identified by the

following questions: "Have you ever heard of the Moral
Majority?" and "If so, how do you feel about the Moral
Majority?"   Respondents were permitted a yes/no response to
the first question and provided space to write in whatever
comments they chose in answer to the second question.   This
open-ended format undoubtedly explained the surprisingly
large amount of obscenities and profanities used to describe
the movement.   Examples of comments we coded as FAVORABLE
are: " [They are] Angels of Mercy·."   or "I am for them." or
"Glad this viewpoint is being brought out for discussion
--- it is a majority view".   Examples of comments coded as
UNFAVORABLE are: "I disagree very strongly with their views
and tactics." or "They are despicable because they try to
force their beliefs on others." or "They are a bunch of ho-
lier-than-thou _____'s".   Finally, comments such
as "I guess it's okay if it's for you." or "I haven't de-
cided yet." were coded as neutral   In addition, respondents
who chose not to comment were coded as neutral or indifferent.   In the interest of avoiding confusion between any
statistical inconsistencies in our report here and on an
earlier paper (Shupe and Stacey, 1982), we note that the
no-comment respondents were not included in that previous
analysis.

   Table 1 presents basic characteristics of the 711 respondents both together and according to their comments on
the Moral Majority.   It is noteworthy that supporters of the
Moral Majority in our Texas sample do not differ significantly from non-supporters and neutrals on most basic social, economic, or demographic characteristics.

TABLE 1: DALLAS-FORT WORTH METROPLEX SAMPLE CHARACTERISTICS*

CHARACTERISTICS	SUPPORTERS OF MORAL MAJORITY	INDIFFERENT TO MORAL MAJORITY	NON-SUPPORTERS OF MORAL MAJ.	TOTAL	
	PERCENT	PERCENT	PERCENT	N	%
Age					
Under 35	41	39	44	288	41
Over 35	59	61	56	422	59
Sex					
Male	51	33	53	297	42
Female	49	67	47	411	58
Education					
H.S. or less	21	44	15	221	31
Some College	44	31	36	246	35
College Grad.	35	25	49	241	34
Income					
Less than 20,000	21	29	21	161	25
20-29,999	18	26	26	158	25
30-39,999	23	19	20	126	20
40,000 or over	38	26	33	191	30
Occupation					
White Collar	60	50	70	389	58
Blue Collar	16	17	11	101	15
Other	24	33	19	185	27
Voting Behavior					
Yes	85	72	88	558	79
No	15	28	12	149	21
Church Attendance					
Seldom	9	19	26	114	20
Now and Then	19	32	17	151	25
Ever Week	72	49	57	334	55

*The number of respondents in all tables will vary slightly because not all persons responded to every item.

The mean age of all respondents is 40.5 years, showing little indication that persons subscribing to the philosophy
of the New Religious Right necessarily represent older Americans. The same is the case for sex and education variables
as well as for income. The high rate of voting overall (85
percent) validates our attempt to seek those persons most
likely to vote and therefore serve as a potential political force or voting bloc behind the Moral Majority. One
noticeable difference among respondents can be seen in the
occupational classification. There are more of the non-
supporters (70 percent) of the Moral Majority holding white-
collar occupations compared to the supporters (60 percent).
Otherwise, demographic and social factors did not prove of
much use in distinguishing supporters from non-supporters
and neutrals.

SCALES

The 78-item questionnaire contained, in addition to
standard social, economic, and demographic questions on respondents' backgrounds, a number of scales measuring congregational and electronic church participation (religiosity), Christian orthodoxy, civil religious sentiments, organizational participation, anti-Catholicism and anti-Semitism. While specific questions will be introduced and
discussed throughout the following chapters, we want to describe the important scales employed.

CIVIL RELIGION SCALE. There has been great interest among
sociologists in the concept of civil religion, particularly since Bellah's (1968) classic essay on the subject. The
Durkheimian notion that secular-political goals and tradi-
tions become blurred with sacred themes has been a useful
and provocative conceptual tool in understanding American

history (e.g., Marty, 1970). A slightly modified version
of the civil religion scale originally developed by Wimberley and his colleagues (see Wimberley, 1979, 1976; Wimberley *et al.*, 1976, for details) was employed to operationa-
lize the civil religion concept after dropping one item
("We should respect the president's authority.") that displayed virtually no dispersion (i.e., discriminatory value)
among respondents. This scale calls for Likert-format responses (Strongly Disagree, Disagree, Agree, Strongly Agree)
with a possible score on each item ranging from 1 to 4
points and summatively scaled with a range of 4 to 20
points. The five items used were:

> I consider holidays such as the 4th of July
> religious as well as patriotic.
> We need more laws on morality.
> National leaders should affirm their be-
> lief in God.
> If the American government does not sup-
> port religion, the government can't up-
> hold morality.
> To me the flag is sacred.

CHRISTIAN ORTHODOXY SCALE. Again, using Likert-format responses, four items taken from Shupe and Wood (1973) were
used to gauge roughly each respondent's degree of Christian
orthodoxy, with a total scale range of 4-16:

> I believe the Bible is the inspired Word
> of God and literally true in all its de-
> tails.
> I believe there are such places as heav-
> en and hell.
> Eternal life is the gift of God only to
> those who believe in Jesus Christ as
> Savior and Lord.

Satan is an actual personality working in
the world today.

CHURCH RELIGIOSITY SCALE. Church religiosity was operationalized by giving a respondent a point if he or she was en-
rolled as a member of a church, another point if he or she
could name its denomination, then points for frequency of
church attendance (3 points for "every week," 2 points for
"only now and then," 1 point for "very seldom," and 0 points
for "not at all") and making financial contributions to the
church (3 points for "at least once a week," 2 points for
"1 or 2 times a month," 1 point for "several times a year,"
and 0 points for "almost never.")

MEDIA RELIGIOSITY SCALE. The media religiosity scale consisted of items measuring frequency of listening to religious radio broadcasts (6 points for "daily," 5 points for
"several times a week," 4 points for "several times a
month," 3 points for "monthly," 2 points for "several times
a year," and 0 points for "never"), frequency of watching
religious broadcasts on television (same points and responses as for listening to religious radio broadcasts), and
frequency of sending in donations or contributions to media
evangelists and programs (4 points for "often," 3 points
for "occasionally," 2 points for "rarely," and 1 point for
"never"). In addition, respondents received 1 point for
each religious television program they could recall watching most frequently.

ANTI-CATHOLICISM AND ANTI-SEMITISM SCALES. As will be discussed in more detail later, there were sufficient reasons
to include in the questionnaire items composing anti-Catholicism and anti-Semitism scales. These were very short and
admittedly crude scales. The items were either constructed

to conform to criteria of face validity or were based
closely on items used in the classic study of prejudice,
The Authoritarian Personality (Adorno et al., 1950).
Three items, using Likert-response format, ranging
1-4 points per question and 4-12 points per scale, were
employed to measure each dimension of prejudice:

ANTI-CATHOLICISM SCALE:
   Catholics make a mistake in placing hu-
   man authority over Biblical authority.
   Catholics' obedience to the Pope makes
   me question their loyalty to the U.S.
   Constitution.
   It is wrong for Protestants and Catho-
   lics to intermarry.

ANTI-SEMITISM SCALE:
   Jewish control in the media, government
   and money matters is out of proportion
   to the number of Jews in the total population.
   The influence of Jewish "intellectuals"
   has probably had a great deal to do
   with the rise of humanism.
   It is wrong for Christians and Jews
   to intermarry.

   These are the core scales of our analysis. Other
measures, mainly clusters of related individual questionnaire items on issues such as secular humanism or evolutionary theory versus creation theory, not combined in scales
will be considered at appropriate places in our discussion
of the 1981 General Population Survey.

THE 1981 DALLAS-FORT WORTH
MINISTERIAL SURVEY

The fall, 1981 Dallas-Fort Worth Ministerial Survey
involved a random sample of 154 Christian clergymen   and
their attitudes toward the New Religious Right (specifically Jerry Falwell's Moral Majority and James Robison's
Religious Roundtable), the electronic church's impact on
local congregations, and various social issues involving
proposed constitutional amendments (specifically school
prayer, abortion, the Equal Rights Amendment, and the teaching of creation theory alongside evolutionary theory). A
total of 160 clergymen (all males) were selected by systematic sampling from all churches listed in the 1980
Southwestern Bell Telephone yellow pages for Dallas and
Fort Worth. After eliminating duplications, 1553 church
congregations (excluding purely administrative and dioce-
san offices) composed the sampling frame. Every eighth
church was selected and contacted by telephone. Assistants
(students in a social research methods training class) were
instructed to call back a maximum of six times if unable to
reach a minister the first call; then, in the event they
could not reach a clergyman, they were provided with an alternate clergyman to contact. Using this sampling by re-
placement procedure, 160 clergymen were directly contacted
and only six refused to be interviewed by telephone, yield-
ing a return rate of 96 percent.

Telephone interviews must be considerably shorter
than conventional face-to-face interviews. Hence the a-
mount of information obtained was not as rich as that of
the General Population Survey. Nevertheless this ministerial survey represented the first attempt to query clergymen of both mainline and sectarian churches as to their
assessments of the impact of the electronic church on

local congregations and their opinions about the Moral Majority. As such, it can compliment the findings gathered
in the larger population and enlarge our understanding of
the potential support base for the New Religious Right. It
is, after all, unlikely that significant numbers of reli-
giously-minded Americans would rally to a Christian movement unaccompanied by clergymen.

The clergymen's denomination breakdown is presented
in Table 2.

TABLE 2: DALLAS-FORT WORTH MINISTERIAL SAMPLE BY
DENOMINATION

	N	%
Fundamentalists (Nazarenes, All Pentecostals, Seventh Day Adventists, All other Non-Southern Baptists)	43	28
Conservatives (Christian/Disciples of Christ, All Lutherans, Church of Christ, Southern Baptist)	60	39
Moderate-to-Liberals (Methodists, Presbyterians, Episcopals)	37	24
Roman Catholics	10	6
Others (Christian Scientists, Mormons, Jehovah's Witnesses)	4	3
Total	154	100

Fifty-four percent had ministered in Texas for 10 years or
longer while 46 percent had ministered there less than 10,
and 26 percent less than 5 years. The level of formal education was relatively high. Only 4 percent had a high
school education or less. Three percent had some college,
22 percent had graduated from college, 76 percent had post-
graduate experience/master's of divinity degree/post-mas-
ter's experience, and 14 percent held doctorates.

SUMMARY

The two 1981 surveys conducted in the Dallas-Fort
Worth Metroplex offer an unique opportunity to assess actual support for the Moral Majority and infusing the political process with conservative Christian morality. They
will also allow us to gauge patterns of electronic church
usage and the latter's relation to conventional congregational participation. Given the Bible-belt location of the
area and the high concentration of fundamentalist and conservative Christians, we believe the two sets of findings
will provide an "acid test" for uncovering whatever grass
roots support for the New Religious Right exists and thus
allow us ultimately to make some prognosis of the New Religious Right's future. Chapters Three to Five analyze the
results of the General Population survey. Chapter Six dis-
cusses results from the Ministerial Survey and highlights
significant comparisons with the General Population Survey.
Chapter Seven offers an overview of what we can infer from
the entire project. The final Chapter Eight offers some
practical consequences of our research as it related to
legislators, clergy, and journalists.

FOOTNOTES

[1]Many of the questions asked personal opinions and probed for religious and political beliefs, hence they were quite sensitive to many respondents. A number of respondents apparently became quite irritated by the questionnaire, suspecting us of either representing the Moral Majority or, alternately, seeking to discredit it. Respondents' refusals to complete the questionnaire were sometimes accompanied by verbal abuse or ripping the questionnaire to shreds on their doorsteps. More than one respondent who did comply took the opportunity to sermonize at length on the back page of the questionnaire about Christian values or our own presumed lack of them for daring to ask others about theirs. In one extreme case a female graduate assistant was confronted by a blue-collar Catholic male who became enraged at our probes for anti-Catholic attitudes and attempted to assault her physically with his fists until she displayed her own St. Christopher's medal. She managed to calm him down long enough to escape to a waiting car. Fortunately she was only shaken up and not injured.

[2]As we indicated in Footnote 1, passions sometimes ran quite strong among respondents who reacted critically to our questionnaire for whatever reason. Likewise, some of the noncompliance -- though certainly not all -- was accompanied by an angry reaction. However, it was the impression of the assistants who encountered such refusals to participate that refusers were as likely to perceive us as representing the Moral Majority as to perceive us as threats to it. Thus we have no reason to believe that we "missed" a significant number of supporters or non-supporters of the Moral Majority.

CHAPTER III

EMPIRICAL PERSPECTIVES ON A NEW
"POLITICAL" MOVEMENT: THE MORAL MAJORITY

America is no stranger to political movements, from
simple lobbying efforts to full-fledged aggregates and categories of citizens (e.g., the anti-war/anti-nuclear power/
environmental/temperance/elderly/feminist groups). Nor are
its citizens strangers to "moral crusaders" (Becker, 1966)
and others who wish to reinstate (or believe they are rein-
stating) lost values and forgotten virtues to government.
It is the latter type of quest that we consider here -- the
Moral Majority as a crusade similar in many ways to what
anthropologist Anthony F.C. Wallace (1966) termed a "revitalization movement," i.e., "a deliberate, organized, con-
scious effort by members of a society to construct a more
satisfying culture." (Such a view, of course, assumes that
the Moral Majority, in its attempt to thwart perceived
threats to its constituency, is creating a definition of
orthodoxy to justify its enterprise rather than simply de-
fending an established, consensually accepted orthodoxy).
In the final chapter we shall consider the implications of
this hypothesis.

29

ABSOLUTE LEVELS OF SUPPORT FOR
THE MORAL MAJORITY

The first and most inescapable finding of the General
Population Survey was the simple tabulating of respondents
according to our unfavorable/neutral/favorable coding
scheme. To begin, *fully 26 percent of the 711 Bible-belt non-
minority respondents claimed they had never heard of the Moral Majority!* Twenty-eight respondents did not respond to the question (i.e., whether or not they had heard of the movement),
but of the remaining 70 percent that had heard of it only
111 (or 16 percent of the total non-minority sample) made
what could be interpreted as favorable or supportive comments about the Moral Majority. Indeed, those holding unfavorable sentiments (220, or 31 percent) outnumber the favorable respondents by two-to-one. The remaining respondents made neutral, non-committal comments.

These results, while in 1981 when they were released
to the media caused a local and even national sensation,
have since been corroborated by national surveys. If anything, our Texas findings *overestimate* support for the
Moral Majority considering national ignorance and indiffer-
ence to it. For example, a *Washington post-ABC News* poll
of 1,533 people revealed that *half* that national sample *had
not heard of the Moral Majority,* and of those who had, *only
one in five* wanted the group to exert more influence in
American life. Conversely, more than 50 percent felt the
Moral Majority's influence needed to be reduced (Peterson
and Sussman, 1980). Similarly, a 1981 Gallup national poll
found that only 40 percent of its 1,551 respondents had
ever heard or read of the Moral Majority and only 26 percent were familiar with its goals and objectives. Disap-
proval of the organizations outweighed approval (among the
relative few who knew of it) by 13 to 8 percent (Gallup,

1981).

Thus, our first critical finding points to a significant parameter of the Moral Majority: its relative unim-
portance to much of the general population, and among those
who know it, its unpopularity.

THE BASIC PHILOSOPHY OF THE MORAL MAJORITY

⌊The political conservatism of the Moral Majority is
based on issues which have been debated in and out of the
courts and by preachers and lay Christians for decades. The
most critical assumption behind Moral Majority positions
seems to be the strong concern with the impact of a trend
toward a secular culture which is affecting the traditional life styles of the conservative right, especially the
church and family.⌋ As Harrell (1981:8) commented on fundamentalist anti-intellectualism, which in many ways is an
earmark of the Moral Majority's critique of both secular humanism and the latter's components such as Darwinian evolutionary theory,

> . . . it was a protest against the chopping up
> of life in the twentieth century. The explosion
> of knowledge, the communication revolution, and
> the endless specialization of modern society
> seemed to rob men of control over their lives,
> giving it over to experts. The intellectual
> protest of conservative religion in the 1920's
> and in the 1970's has been aimed at what many
> common people believe to be scientific elitism
> which encroaches on their right to make re-
> ligious choices and to nurture their children
> in their beliefs.

Thus⌊we identified three interrelated general dimensions of the "world view" expressed by the proponents of the

Moral Majority. These three interrelated dimensions involved the issues of "values clarification" (i.e., teaching adolescents to sort out personal, rather than strictly
biblical, priorities for responsible decision-making on al-
cohol/tobacco,/drug use/ premarital sex), "secular humanism" (i.e., so-called human-centered rather than God-cen-
tered morality), and general humanistic perspectives
(loosely interpreted as atheism) perceived to be the product of the educational system. Table 3 demonstrates the
attitudes of the supporters, non-supporters, and neutrals
with regard to these dimensions.

TABLE 3:   HUMANISTIC VALUES AND SUPPORT FOR THE MORAL
MAJORITY

BASIC ASSUMPTIONS	SUPPORTERS OF MORAL MAJORITY		INDIFFERENT TOWARDS MOR- AL MAJORITY		NON-SUPPORTERS OF MORAL MA- JORITY	
	N	%	N	%	N	%
1. Secular Human- ism Undermines Christianity						
Agree	79	80	141	56	65	34
Disagree	20	20	111	44	126	66
2. Values Clarifi- cation should be a part of every school curricu- lum						
Agree	77	81	269	86	155	78
Disagree	18	19	43	14	43	22
3. One of the major problems in educ. today is that sec. humanists have been allowed to det. the textbooks used in the public school system						
Agree	81	80	148	58	71	37
Disagree	20	20	107	42	119	63

We expected strong support in our sample, particularly among supporters of the Moral Majority, for the basic
premises of the Moral Majority and its generally anti-secu-
lar attitudes. In the item "Secular humanism undermines
Christianity" 80 percent of the supporters of the Moral Majority agreed while 66 percent of the non-supporters of the
Moral Majority disagreed with this statement. This is not
surprising. As Jorstad (1981:111) noted particularly with
regard to the large number of evangelicals active in the
New Religious Right:

> They find in secular humanism the enemy the
> staunch conservatives of the 1950's found in
> political and religious liberalism -- the
> means by which the sacred elements in Amer-
> ican life created by God are being under-
> mined; what is wrong with America today
> is traceable to secular humanism.

Closely related is the view that "Secular humanists
have been allowed to determine textbooks used in the public
schools." Again supporters of the political right agreed
(80 percent) compared to non-supporters (37 percent). The
surprising finding involved values clarification where 81
percent of the supporters of the Moral Majority agreed that
values clarification should be taught in the public schools.
This finding is directly opposed to what we anticipated.
After all, values clarification, as an outgrowth of humanistic philosophy, has been one of the most vehemently at-
tacked issues in the conservative campaign of local Texas
evangelist James Robison. Robison and Falwell both have
maintained that values clarification should be a joint product of the home and church since public shcools are perceived as requiring secular humanistic values, which are
construed as essentially atheistic and thus detrimental to
the traditional family orientation. Either one of two

interpretations of this high support for teaching values
clarification may be considered: (1) that the self-defined supporters of the Moral Majority disagree with the
movement's political leadership, indicating devisiveness,
or: (2) the leadership of the conservative right is simply not getting its message to their supporters, i.e., many
persons who say they support the Moral Majority do not have
the faintest idea what the "values clarification" issue is
all about. In either case the consensus of supporters on
this fundamental New Religious Right issue has to be seriously questioned.

KEY SOCIO-POLITICAL ISSUES AND SUPPORT
FOR THE MORAL MAJORITY

The social and political issues that have been addressed by the Moral Majority are of major importance since
they provide a rallying point for the party. These issues
include abortion, women's rights, sex education in public
schools, evolution theory versus creation theory, and prayer in public schools. Table 4 summarizes the relationships
between the attitudes of respondents on these issues and
their support for the New Religious Right.

TABLE 4: BASIC ISSUES OF THE MORAL MAJORITY

ISSUES	SUPPORTERS OF MORAL MAJORITY		INDIFFERENT TOW. MOR. MAJ.		NON-SUPPORTERS OF MOR. MAJ.	
	N	%	N	%	N	%
1. Abortion is a sin against God's law						
Agree 73		66	188	54	80	40
Disagree 37		34	157	46	122	60

TABLE 4:   BASIC ISSUES OF THE MORAL MAJORITY (CONT.)

ISSUES	SUPPORTERS OF MORAL MAJORITY		INDIFFERNT TOW. MOR. MAJ.		NON-SUPPORTERS OF MOR. MAJ.	
	N	%	N	%	N	%
2. I believe in ERA to guar. women equal rights						
Agree	44	41	271	75	137	64
Disagree	63	59	88	25	75	35
3. Evolution should be taught in school						
Agree	50	46	196	56	172	81
Disagree	58	54	153	44	41	19
4. The Biblical account of creation should be taught in school						
Agree	84	88	249	74	128	64
Disagree	11	12	86	26	73	36
5. I think prayer should be allowed in school						
Agree	104	95	333	90	163	78
Disagree	5	5	36	10	47	22
6. Sex education should be taught in the schools						
Agree	67	62	296	82	186	88
Disagree	41	38	64	18	26	12

Perhaps the most frequently mentioned and publicized issues involve the U.S. Supreme Court's 1973 decision on abortion. This decision is still being heatedly debated

among all segments of the population.⌝ As Jorstad (1981:77)
has observed: "Without any doubt, the most controversial
and least compromisable issue regarding human sexuality is
that of abortion. No issue in the 70's divided Americans
more bitterly, none has had so drastic an effect on American life." One recent public debate in the Dallas-Fort
Worth Metroplex between Phyllis Schlafley and a former president of the National Organization of Women for example,
intimated that a public referendum should be called since a
few select men (The 1981 Supreme Court) made the decision
to·legalize abortion without reference to popular opinion.
Even though a matter of law is not subject to popular (or
unpopular, as the conservative right maintains) opinion, a
large number of people in America are involved in a pro-life
movement.⌝ This movement began when the Supreme Court's decision was first rendered and has recently been identified
as the major legislative issue of the political platform of
the Moral Majority. In order to determine the relationship
between political ideology and the issue of abortion it was
hypothesized that respondents supportive of the New Religious Right would certainly be against the Supreme Court's
decision which does not provide legal protection for an un-
born fetus.⌝ It is apparent from Table 4 that among the supporters of the Moral Majority a substantial number (66 percent) agree with the pro-life position compared to non-supporters (40 percent). This finding was anticipated but surprisingly 34 percent of the supporters of the political
right dissent from this most basic and sensitive political
issue of the political platform of the Moral Majority. To
reiterate, the basic premise of the political platform of
the Moral Majority, according to repeated statement by
founder Jerry Falwell, is one of anti-abortion. It would
appear from these data that a significant proportion of the
persons claiming membership in or who philosophically

support the political platform of the Moral Majority are at variance with a fundamental aspect of the new religious right.

A second issue implicit in the platform of the Moral Majority involves a pro-traditional family perspective. A pro-traditional family orientation must necessarily include the traditional status of women in society. The traditional role and status of women has been the subjugation of women in the family, economic exploitation of women in the labor force outside the home, and women playing inferior roles in politics, education and religion. Since the political platform of the Moral Majority is highly conservative and thus supports the traditional role of women in American society it was hypothesized that supporters of the political platform of the new religious right would be against the Equal Rights Amendment for women.

Since the data supports the basic premise of the supporters of the Moral Majority, several observations are needed for purposes of clarification and not to mislead the reader. First we point out that 452 or 67 percent of the total sample agree that passage of the Equal Rights Amendment is necessary to guarantee equal rights for women. These percentages correspond favorably to data collected in other areas of the nation with respect to support for ERA. Second, 79 percent of the sample voted in the November, 1980 election. Among those voting 68 percent supported Reagan even though his political platform was conservative and explicitly denounced the ERA. Most political analysts agree that single issue politics are not accepted by the voting populace. On the other hand, one would anticipate those persons expressing support for the Moral Majority would be supportive of the pro-traditional family platform. Ironically a considerable 41 percent of the pro-Moral Majority supporters feel that the Equal Rights Amendment is needed

to guarantee equal rights for women in American society.
Thus, a political party which advocates traditional domestic status for over one-half of the nation's population may
discover one day that among its rank and file membership
that there is divisiveness.

⌠Several issues central to the pro-traditionalist family orientation of the Moral Majority concern their views on
education and the role of the public school system. It is
apparent that many in the New Religious Right feel that much
of the change in American society is a result of an emerging secular culture that has resulted from educational experiences of their children.⌡ In a recent article Lorentzen
(1980) stated that:

> Apprehension and even outrage were expressed at
> the influences that bear upon children. The
> family is not only a protective environment
> in which to rear children but it is also the
> stage for socialization to the evangelical
> faith. Secular influences, at times, were
> seen as contrary to this process, *especially*
> *those influences that are institutionalized*
> *in the public schools.*

There are basically four expressed concerns of the
evangelical right on the subject of public school. Their
concerns include the teaching of evolution theory as scientific fact, the absence of creation theory as an alternative, the absence of prayer in the school and opposition to
sex education as part of the school curriculum. As expected, Table 4 indicates that a larger percentage of the
New Religious Right disagree with the scientific explanation of evolution, agree with teaching the Biblical concept
of creation, and feel that prayer should be allowed in
school. Yet surprisingly, a very high percentage (62 percent) agreed that sex education should be taught in school.

One might infer that their earlier response on values clarification possibly was a misunderstanding; here on sex education however, it is rather unlikely. Similar evidence of
a lack of consensus can be seen in the fact that a significant proportion (46 percent) of supporters want the scientific theory taught in schools. We can conclude from inspecting responses to the third and fourth issue items that
many supporters may prefer creation theory to evolutionary
theory but do not wish to see the former taught to the ex-
clusion of the latter.

 We also tested for the strength of the relationships
between support for the Moral Majority and each of the issues identified as important to the views on secularization,
basic issues of the political platform of the Moral Majority, and civil religion. Table 5 displays these relationships.

TABLE 5: CHI-SQUARE AND GAMMA VALUES FOR THE STRENGTH OF
     THE RELATIONSHIP BETWEEN SUPPORT FOR THE MORAL
     MAJORITY AND KEY ISSUES

ISSUE	x^2	GAMMA VALUE	P-VALUE
Humanism undermines Christian-ity	90.2	-.46	.001
Values clarification	25.6	-.17	.01
Secular textbooks	86.4	+.46	.001
Abortion	80.8	-.25	.001
ERA	73.5	+.17	.01
Evolution	89.0	+.42	.001
Creation	45.4	-.32	.001
Prayer	72.7	-.45	.001
Sex Education	38.9	+.30	.001
Civil Religion Scale	62.0	-.43	.001
Religion and Politics	81.8	-.44	.001

The chi-square and Gamma values are significant, indicating
moderate to strong relationships.

To this point our analysis has demonstrated that the
supporters of the Moral Majority are divided on basic phil-
osophical issues and socio-political issues. Moreover,
there has been some speculation as to the religious composition of supporters of the Moral Majority. Indeed, Falwell has insisted vociferously that his is a political and
not a religious movement, that it represents a broad spec-
trum of various Protestant and sectarian Christian denominations, Jews, and Catholics. Thus he stated that the Moral Majority "is a political organization" (Falwell, 1981b)
and that "The Moral Majority is not a Christian or a religious organization. . ." (Falwell, 1981a:17). He added:

> I suppose that the No. 1 misconception about
> the Moral Majority is that it is a religious
> organization. It is not. It is totally a
> political organization . . . . We must al-
> ways prevent Moral Majority from becoming
> religious. In fact, the day it does, it
> will die. There is no religious agree-
> ment inside the organization.

Table 6 tests this assertion.

TABLE 6: THE RELATIONSHIP BETWEEN DENOMINATION AND SUPPORT
FOR THE MORAL MAJORITY

MORAL MAJORITY	FUNDAMENTAL		CONSERVATIVE		MODERATE	
	N	%	N	%	N	%
Supporters	22	29	44	19	23	14
Indifferent	46	62	134	56	84	52
Non-supporters	7	9	60	25	56	34
Totals	75	100.0	238	100.0	163	100.0

$x^2 = 22.6$ $V = .15$ $Pr < .001$

The data show that among fundamentalists 29 percent
are supporters while only 19 percent and 14 percent of the
conservative and moderate denominations, respectively, tend
to support the Moral Majority. Support, in other words,
tends to be more noticeably concentrated among religious
fundamentalists. Falwell's claim of broad inter-denomina-
tion representation among grass roots supporters is further
belied by considering the Roman Catholic subsample. Here
we found that out of the 110 Catholics surveyed only 10 indicated positive sentiments toward the Moral Majority.

THE MORAL MAJORITY AND RELIGIOUS PREJUDICE

Jerry Falwell, as we have seen, purports the Moral
Majority to be a non-sectarian lobbying effort. Within the
past year he has also received accolades from leaders in
Israel because of his outspoken support for that nation as
well as (by his own account) from prominent leaders in the
American Jewish community. In addition, Falwell frequently
mentions the endorsements of leaders in the Catholic Church.
We do not question the authenticity of these supportive activities of persons from non-Protestant religious groups.
We do, however, ask if the grass roots supporters of the
Moral Majority's platform share Falwell's sentiments regarding Catholics and Jews. Our reason for probing for
anti-Catholic and anti-Semitic attitudes in our general sample originally arose from the experiences of a graduate stu-
dent colleague who attended meetings of the Christian Wom-
en's National Concerns group. This organization is an aux-
iliary of the Fort Worth-based Religious Roundtable and is
coordinated by both evangelist James Robison's wife and the
wife of Fort Worth millionaire Cullen T. Davis. At these
meetings our colleague reported to us having heard anti-
Catholic remarks made in conversations. Since past research

(e.g., Adorno *et al.*, 1950) has found anti-Semitic prejudice to be associated with anti-Catholic and other exclu-
sionary attitudes, we included several question-items in
our General Population Survey questionnaire.

The data in Tables 7 and 8 identify an inconsistency
between the leaders of the Moral Majority and those persons
who claim to support the movement's platform with regard to
attitudes about Catholics and Jews.

TABLE 7:   RELATIONSHIP BETWEEN SUPPORT FOR THE MORAL
           MAJORITY AND ANTI-SEMITISM USING CHI-SQUARE
           DISTRIBUTIONS

ANTI-SEMITIC ATTITUDES	SUPPORTERS OF MORAL MAJ.		NEUTRAL OR NO COMMENT		NON-SUPPORTERS OF MOR. MAJ.	
	N	%	N	%	N	%
Low	65	59	290	76	160	73
Moderate	35	31	71	19	50	23
High	11	10	18	5	10	4
Total	111	100.0	379	100.0	220	100.0

x^2 = 14.9   V = .10   Pr = .004

TABLE 8:   RELATIONSHIP BETWEEN SUPPORT FOR THE MORAL
           MAJORITY AND ANTI-CATHOLICISM USING CHI-
           SQUARE DISTRIBUTIONS

ANTI-CATHOLIC ATTITUDES	SUPPORTERS OF MORAL MAJ.		NEUTRAL OR NO COMMENT		NON-SUPPORTERS OF MOR. MAJ.	
	N	%	N	%	N	%
Low	58	52	270	71	163	74
Moderate	34	31	79	21	47	21
High	19	17	30	8	10	5
Total	111	100.0	379	100.0	220	100.0

x^2 = 23.6   V = .13   Pr = .0001

The data presented in the previous two tables represent the responses of 711 non-minority respondents from the
Dallas-Fort Worth metropolitan area. Among the supporters
of the Moral Majority we found that 10 percent were high in
anti-Semitism while only 5 percent of the non-supporters
were high. When moderate and high levels of anti-Semitism
are combined among the supporters of the Moral Majority, an
amazing 40 percent show some to strong agreement with anti-
Semitic sentiments (as compared to one-fourth of the non-
supporters). The difference between supporters and non-
supporters is statistically significant.

The data presented in Table 8 show a stronger relationship between support for the Moral Majority and anti-
Catholicism than between such support and anti-Semitism.
Among the supporters of the Moral Majority 17 percent are
high in anti-Catholic sentiments while among the non-supporters only 5 percent feel this way about Catholics.
Again, if we combine moderate with high anti-Catholic categories, almost one-half (48 percent) of the supporters of
the Moral Majority have moderate to strong negative feelings
about Catholics in this area as compared to one-fourth of
the non-supporters. While the leadership of the Moral Majority may proclaim that its political platform is non-sectarian and receives broad inter-denominational support, in-
spection of the grass roots supporters does not validate
that claim. Catholics in particular, as we noted earlier,
are low in supporting the Moral Majority, and in turn many
supporters of the Moral Majority movement show clear signs
of being anti-Catholic. Exploring anti-Catholic and anti-
Semitic sentiments further, we analyzed the relationship between church denomination and the two types of prejudice.
Table 9 contains data relevant to this phase of the analysis, displaying a clear relationship between anti-Catholicism and religious denomination. (A similar analysis of

the relation between denomination and anti-Semitism was
not statistically significant, though there were twice as
many fundamentalists who agreed with anti-Semitic statements as moderates, i.e., 9 percent compared to 4 percent.)

TABLE 9: THE RELATIONSHIP BETWEEN RELIGIOUS DENOMINATION
          AND ANTI-CATHOLICISM USING THE CHI-SQUARE AND
          GAMMA DISTRIBUTIONS

ANTI-CATHOLIC ATTITUDES	FUNDAMENTAL DENOMINATIONS		CONSERVATIVE DENOMINATIONS		MODERATE DENOMINATIONS	
	N	%	N	%	N	%
Low	39	46	146	57	132	79
Moderate	28	33	79	31	31	18
High	18	21	32	12	5	3
Total	85	100.0	257	100.0	168	100.0

$x^2 = 38.4$ $V = .19$ $Pr = .0001$

As Table 9 shows, anti-Catholic sentiments are more frequently found in the fundamentalist denominations; anti-
Catholicism shrinks as one moves toward the moderates, i.e.,
from 54 percent to 21 percent. Given the former groups'
traditional antipathy toward ecumenical activities and in
particular to the entire Christian institution in Rome,
this finding is not surprising. We may also be tapping, to
an unknown extent, ethnic hostility. Slightly over 10 percent of the total population in the Dallas-Fort Worth Metroplex is Mexican-American, most of whom are Roman Catholics,
and the issue of illegal Mexican aliens (of which there were
an estimated 100,000 in this location alone) was a volatile
one at the time of our survey. Thus some of the anti-Catholic sentiment may also reflect anti-Mexican prejudice.

SUMMARY

Our survey of middle-class home-owning white Texans
in the Dallas-Fort Worth Metroplex has revealed a number
of qualifications as to who supports the New Religious
Right as represented by Jerry Falwell's Moral Majority.

First, and perhaps most dramatic, the Moral Majority
commands low support among the public at large. Indeed,
Falwell's detractors outnumber his supporters two-to-one.
A fourth of our sample had not even heard of the Moral Majority.

Second, on specific issues such as abortion, the Equal
Rights Amendment, prayer in public schools, and sex education in schools there is no united bloc of supporters, i.e.,
even among those who claim to support the Moral Majority
there is no consensus on important issues.

Third, despite claims of Moral Majority support among
all religious groups and expressions of goodwill to non-
Protestants, grass roots supporters of the Moral Majority
are more likely than either neutrals or non-supporters to
agree with anti-Semitic and anti-Catholic statements. This
fact is not a major revelation once the basic fundamentalist
Christian composition of the Moral Majority's grass roots
supporters is established.

CHAPTER IV

THE MORAL MAJORITY: RELIGIOUS
OR POLITICAL MOVEMENT?

Not long after initial findings from the 1981 General
Population Survey were picked up by the print and video media, Fort Worth evangelist James Robison denounced the study
(and us personally) in the *Fort Worth Star-Telegram* (10/26/
81), saying "it is time for the preachers to get involved --
I am taking 1,000 preachers to Washington and teach them the
art of politics." Soon after Robison appeared as a guest
preacher on Jerry Falwell's *Old Time Gospel Hour* and vehemently criticized his fellow clergymen for their lack of
initiative and involvement in spreading Christian morality.
The thrust of his message (which we shall return to in Chapter Six when we examine clergymen) was that most clergy lack
either the political sophistication or the courage to take
their demands for greater morality in laws and policies to
politicians.

What we might tentatively infer from all this is that
persons who admire and support New Religious Right leaders
and organizations, specifically those connected with the
electronic church, not only belong to fundamentalist/con-
servative denominations (which as we have shown is true) but
also (1) tend to be themselves high in religious orthodoxy,

(2) feel that religious values should be infused into gov-
ernmental policies (i.e., morality should be legislated to
some extent) with strong sentiments of civil religion, and
(3) are personally active in religious activities. These
latter activities, we might further expect, would include
not only conventional congregational religiosity (participation) but also consuming radio and television programming
(i.e., the electronic church). The purpose of this chapter
is to investigate these logical extensions of the findings
in Chapter Three, with the goal of answering the question,
"Is the Moral Majority primarily a political or a religious
movement?"

CIVIL RELIGION AND THE MORAL MAJORITY

Moral Majority founder Jerry Falwell has reiterated
often that the political goal of the Moral Majority is to
"line people up -- at the polls"/(see, e.g., *Newsweek,*
September 21, 1981). The current era is certainly not the
first time in the history of the United States that religious groups have been politically active. But to what extent do those persons who might line up in support of the
Moral Majority hold attitudes suggesting a strong civil religious orientation? In order to consider the relationship
between support for the Moral Majority and beliefs about the
extent that religion should be involved in the political
process, a six-item civil religion scale was administered to
the respondents adapted from Wimberley, *et al.,* 1976). In
addition, a seventh over-all item measuring sympathy for organized religious involvement in politics was included (but
not as part of the civil religion scale). The frequencies
and percentages of responses are displayed in Table 10.

TABLE 10:   CIVIL RELIGION AMONG SUPPORTERS AND NON-SUPPORT-
ERS OF THE MORAL MAJORITY

STATEMENT	SUPPORTERS OF MORAL MAJORITY		INDIFFERENT TOW. MOR. MAJ.		NON-SUPPORTERS OF MORAL MAJ.	
	N	%	N	%	N	%
1. I consider holidays such as the 4th of July religious as well as patriotic						
Agree	29	27	69	20	16	8
Disagree	79	73	275	80	197	92
2. We need more laws on morality.						
Agree	68	65	220	63	40	19
Disagree	36	35	132	37	171	81
3. National leaders should affirm their belief in God.						
Agree	88	81	256	73	93	45
Disagree	21	19	95	27	114	55
4. If the Amer. govt. does not support religion, the govt. can't uphold morality						
Agree	55	54	212	61	52	25
Disagree	46	46	136	39	153	75
5. We should respect pres. authority.						
Agree	108	97	342	96	196	92
Disagree	3	3	14	4	17	8
6. To me the flag is sacred.						
Agree	75	70	281	80	115	55
Disagree	32	30	69	20	96	45
7. I think religion should be involved in politics.*						
Agree	64	62	114	34	37	17
Disagree	39	38	226	66	175	83

*Not included in the Civil Religion Scale

Responses to the seven civil religion items show significant differences among the three types of respondents.
The most conservative respondents obviously are the supporters of the Moral Majority. However, key issues among
civil religion advocates include the "need for more laws on
morality" and the feeling that "if the American government
does not support religion, the government cannot uphold
morality." We find a great deal of dispersion among the
supporters of the Moral Majority. An especially interesting finding is that 38 percent of the supporters did not
feel that religion should be involved in the political process. This much divisiveness among the supporters of the
Moral Majority on the issue of religion's involvement in
politics suggests that many such persons approve of the ab-
stract concept of greater morality in politics and perceive
a sacred dimension in the secular political tradition, but
they do not necessarily endorse the intrusion of formal organized religion into political parties, groups, or legislation. In other words, some respondents supportive of the
Moral Majority may applaud the general notion of more morality in politics, but they stop short -- whether out of
consideration for keeping church and state separate or for
whatever reason -- of agreeing that religion *per se* should
directly influence political decisions.

Combining the first six statements additively into a
civil religion scale allows us to test more directly the
relationship between civil religion and support for the Moral Majority. Table 11 presents these findings.

TABLE 11:   THE RELATIONSHIP BETWEEN SUPPORT FOR THE MORAL
            MAJORITY AND CIVIL RELIGION USING CHI-SQUARE
            AND GAMMA DISTRIBUTIONS

CIVIL RELIGION	SUPPORTERS OF MOR. MAJ.		INDIFFERENT TOW. MOR. MAJ.		NON-SUPPORTERS OF M.M.	
	N	%	N	%	N	%
Low	21	19	95	25	115	52
Medium	53	48	186	49	88	40
High	37	33	98	26	17	8
Total	111	100.0	379	100.0	220	100.0

x^2 = 71.9   V = .23   Pr. = .0001

As anticipated, the relationship is statistically significant. Among the supporters of the Moral Majority 33
percent were high in civil religion while only 8 percent of
the non-supporters felt this way. Thus we conclude that
supporters of the Moral Majority tend to have internalized
a perspective on politics that justifies infusing their
Christian morality into the political arena, though as we
have noted, this view is far from unanimous. Strong civil
religious sentiments, in other words, cannot be simply equat-
ed with condoning religious lobbying in politics. Taken
one step further, we cannot automatically assume strong civil religious sentiments to be evidence of support for direct
political action. The further question that this finding
poses is, What *are* the factors that contribute to mobilizing a desire to integrate religion and politics? The remainder of this chapter seeks to answer this question.

CHURCH RELIGIOSITY AND SUPPORT FOR
THE MORAL MAJORITY

Thusfar evidence has shown that members of fundamentalist and conservative denominations are more likely to be
supporters of the Moral Majority. And given both the frequently intense-to-strong demands for church participation
as well as evangelicals' own claims to be reinforcing and
encouraging local church attendance (e.g., Armstrong, 1979),
it is logical to hypothesize that as church religiosity in-
creases so will support for the Moral Majority. Table 12
provides a test of this assumption.

TABLE 12:   THE RELATIONSHIP BETWEEN CHURCH RELIGIOSITY AND
            SUPPORT FOR THE MORAL MAJORITY USING CHI-SQUARE
            DISTRIBUTIONS

CHURCH RELIGIOSITY	SUPPORTERS OF M.M.		INDIFFERENT TOW. M.M.		NON-SUPPORT-ERS OF M.M.	
	N	%	N	%	N	%
Low	14	13	96	25	41	19
High	97	87	243	75	179	81
Total	111	100.0	379	100.0	220	100.0

x^2 = 9.61   Pr. = .008   V = .12

Though the hypothesis is supported by the data, i.e.,
church religiosity is positively and significantly associated with support for the Moral Majority, the overall relationship is not strong. A partial explanation may be that
an unusually high percentage of the total sample is high
in church religiosity, just as it is in voting and other
activities. Had our goal in this study not originally been
to locate supporters of the Moral Majority, hence less pur-
posive, we would expect the relation between the two

variables in, say, a more general cross-sectional sample, to be much stronger.

RELIGIOUS ORTHODOXY AND SUPPORT
FOR THE MORAL MAJORITY

As we noted earlier, previous findings show that religious denomination is significantly related to support for the Moral Majority. It is among the fundamentalists that we find the strongest support. The concept of religious orthodoxy is operationalized here in such a way that it is an index of the extent to which a person employs a literal interpretation of the Bible. We hypothesized that the Moral Majority, whose leadership is composed primarily of fundamentalist and conservative Christians, would appeal more to persons high in religious orthodoxy rather than to persons with more liberal views. Since denominations are traditionally understood by sociologists to represent clusters of not only organizational differences but also theological ones, we hypothesized that support for the Moral Majority would be significantly related to religious orthodoxy, with such support receding as one moved from fundamentalist to moderate denominations. Table 13 displays this relationship.

TABLE 13: THE RELATIONSHIP BETWEEN RELIGIOUS ORTHODOXY AND SUPPORT FOR THE MORAL MAJORITY USING CHI-SQUARE AND GAMMA DISTRIBUTIONS

RELIGIOUS ORTHODOXY	SUPPORTERS OF MOR. MAJ.		INDIFFERENT TOW. M.M.		NON-SUPPORTERS OF MOR. MAJ.	
	N	%	N	%	N	%
Low	13	12	52	14	78	35
Medium	12	11	115	30	68	31
High	86	77	212	56	74	34
Totals	1̅1̅1	1̅0̅0.0	3̅7̅9̅	1̅0̅0.0	2̅2̅0	1̅0̅0.0

x^2 = 79.6   V = .24   Pr. = .001

Table 13 reveals that religious orthodoxy is significantly
related to support for the Moral Majority. Among the supporters of the Moral Majority, 77 percent are high in religious orthodoxy as compared to 56 and 34 percent of the
neutrals and non-supporters, respectively. This is consistent both with our earlier finding that fundamentalist
Christians are more likely to support the Moral Majority and
with the fundamentalist/conservative biblical posture of such
New Religious Right leaders as Jerry Falwell and James Robison.

MEDIA RELIGIOSITY AND SUPPORT FOR

THE MORAL MAJORITY

The Moral Majority has made extensive use of all media in seeking to broadcast its message and appeals for support. Undoubtedly the most controversial medium used by
this movement has been the electronic one, or as Hadden and
Swann (1981) term the phenomenon, "televangelism". We used
the label "electronic church" as a euphemism for radio and
television religious programming that is often evangelical
Christian in orientation. (It is a variation on the ori-
ginal term "electric church" first coined by Ben Armstrong,
1979). Since the Moral Majority and the leaders of the New
Religious Right are inextricably related to the electronic
church, it is worth briefly commenting on the latter phenomenon to set the context of our findings in this section.
There is little question that since the first regular religious broadcasts on Pittsburgh radio station KDKA
in 1920, and particularly within the last 10-15 years, religious programming in the United States has mushroomed.
Mariani (1979:22-25) mentioned over 25 television stations
now almost totally religious in program content. By itself
the Christian Broadcasting Network, founded by evangelist

and religious talk show host Pat Robertson, broadcasts to
over 4,000 cable stations, 60 satellite stations, and 130
commercial stations. Moreover, of the approximately 8,700
radio stations currently operating in the United States,
1,400 (or 15 percent) are classified as predominantly religious by the Federal Communications Commission (*Fort
Worth Star-Telegram,* February 2, 1980). Armstrong (1979:56)
claimed there are six hundred radio stations that broadcast
exclusively religious programs and are owned by evangelical
Christians. There has even been recent evidence that mainline denominations, which have traditionally enjoyed free
airtime reserved by the Federal Communications Commission,
are also expanding their electronic missions to keep pace
with the evangelicals. For example, The Communications
Committee of the United States Catholic Conference has been
studying the technical feasibility of establishing its
own telecommunications system, as have also the United Pres-
byterian Church in the U.S.A. and the Methodist General Conference (e.g., Lovelace, 1981).

The long-range implications and significance of the
electronic church particularly as it affects conventional
congregations and denominations, have been subjects of
concerned debate among mainline organizations such as the
National Council of Churches of Christ. As yet it remains
a debate confounded by contradictory inferences and claims.
For example, "electric church" apologist Armstrong (1979:9)
maintains that the recent aggressive programming expansion
of certain evangelical corporations and preachers is due
not only to their tenacity and skill but also to the superi-
ority of their conservative Christian message. He affirmed:
"I believe that God has raised up this powerful technology
of radio and television expressly to reach every man, woman,
boy, and girl on earth with the even more powerful message
of the gospel". Armstrong also asserted that the electronic

church reinforces local church attendance and membership:
    The electric church is not a replacement for
    the local assembly of believers but a comple-
    ment to it (p. 10).
and   Contrary to the critics' allegations, reli-
    gious radio and television enhances church
    attendance, financial support, and spiritual
    growth (p. 144).
Armstrong accused critics of the electronic church of being
merely invidious (liberal) detractors.

Using Nielson ratings data, sociologist William Martin (1981:11-12) debunked the myth that various evangelists
such as Jerry Falwell and Oral Roberts can actually rely on
the tens (and, they sometimes boast, hundreds) of millions
of supporters that they claim but concurred that most of
the more modest 7-10 million total audience for media religion is made up of active church members.

Nevertheless, the evangelical electronic church has
been accused of siphoning off both participating members
and financial contributions from local churches. For example, in February, 1980 the National Council of Churches
of Christ and the United States Catholic Conference met in
New York to discuss just these putative problems. Johnson
(1979) has criticized the electronic church for its commercial slickness in almost nonstop fund raising, its super-
ficial theology, and its failure to provide the personal
solace and support that only a local clergyman and congregation can. There have been other dimensions to the controversy, such as the alleged simplistic discussion of complex
economic and political issues on upbeat, colorful talk shows
(e.g., the 700 Club and the PTL Club) and the thinly veiled
ethnocentric promotion of American civil religion. To all
such charges "televangelist" Robert Schuller, undoubtedly
speaking for many of his colleagues, counter-criticized the

mainline denominations for making the electronic pastors
whipping boys for their own declining memberships and in-
adequacies:

> At the deepest levels, the mainline denomi-
> nations, Catholic and Protestant, are running
> scared . . . . They are failing to meet the
> deepest emotional needs of the people. Ob-
> viously we are meeting profound needs or we'd
> be out of business. (*Fort Worth Star-Telegram*,
> February 17, 1980).

The dependence of "televangelists" like Falwell and
Robison on the electronic media led us to predict that in-
dividuals high in media religiosity would be more likely to
support the Moral Majority. The data displayed in Table 14
support this hypothesis. Among the supporters of the Moral

TABLE 14:   THE RELATIONSHIP BETWEEN SUPPORT FOR THE MORAL
            MAJORITY AND MEDIA RELIGIOSITY USING CHI-SQUARE
            AND GAMMA DISTRIBUTIONS

MEDIA RELIGIOSITY	SUPPORTERS		NEUTRALS		NON-SUPPORTERS	
	N	%	N	%	N	%
Low	40	36	251	66	179	81
Medium	24	22	71	19	31	14
High	47	42	57	15	10	5
Total	111	100.0	379	100.0	220	100.0

$x^2 = 91.9$ $V = .25$ Pr. = .0001

Majority, 42 percent scored high on media religiosity as
compared to neutrals and non-supporters who scored high on
media religiosity 15 and 5 percent, respectively.

THE DENOMINATIONAL DETERMINANT

Thusfar we have found that church religiosity, religious orthodoxy, civil religion, and media religiosity are all significantly related to support for the Moral Majority. An emerging picture of the Moral Majority's grass roots support base shows it to be fundamentalist/conservative in religious orthodoxy, frequent in church attendance, high in civil religious sentiments, and strong in consumption of (and support for) the electronic church. We also know from previous analysis in Chapter Three that denominational affiliation is a significant correlate of support for the Moral Majority.

However, in order to obtain a more definitive answer to the question we introduced at the beginning of this chapter (i.e., "Is the Moral Majority primarily a political or a religious movement?"), we need to examine further the interrelatedness of denomination with the civil religion, religious orthodoxy, and media religiosity variables. Tables 15, 16, and 17 display denomination's relationship to these three variables.

TABLE 15: THE RELATIONSHIP BETWEEN DENOMINATION AND CIVIL
RELIGION USING CHI-SQUARE AND GAMMA DISTRIBUTIONS

CIVIL RELIGION	FUNDAMENTAL		CONSERVATIVE		MODERATE	
	N	%	N	%	N	%
Low	9	12	45	19	38	23
Medium	23	31	132	55	96	59
High	43	57	61	26	30	18
Total	75	100.0	238	100.0	164	100.0

$x^2 = 41.6$ $V = .21$ $Pr = .0001$

TABLE 16: THE RELATIONSHIP BETWEEN DENOMINATION AND RELI-
GIOUS ORTHODOXY USING CHI-SQUARE AND GAMMA
DISTRIBUTIONS

CHRISTIAN ORTHO-DOXY	FUNDAMENTAL		CONSERVATIVE		MODERATE	
	N	%	N	%	N	%
Low	2	3	22	9	48	29
Medium	12	16	58	24	57	35
High	61	81	158	67	59	36
Total	75	100.0	238	100.0	164	100.0

$X^2 = 69.0$ $V = .27$ $Pr = .0001$

TABLE 17: THE RELATIONSHIP BETWEEN DENOMINATION AND MEDIA
RELIGIOSITY USING THE CHI-SQUARE AND GAMMA DIS-
TRIBUTIONS

MEDIA RELIGIOSITY	FUNDAMENTAL		CONSERVATIVE		MODERATE	
	N	%	N	%	N	%
Low	28	37	140	59	117	71
High	47	63	98	41	47	29
Total	75	100.0	238	100.0	164	100.0

$X^2 = 25.6$ $V = .16$ $Pr = .0001$

The data in Tables 15,16, and 17 show quite conclusively that most of the support for the Moral Majority de-
rives from the fundamentalist sector of our sample. That is
what we refer to as the *denomination determinant* of such
support. For example, in Table 15, 57 percent of the fundamentalists scored high on civil religion; in Table 16, 81
percent of the fundamentalists scored high on religious orthodoxy; and in Table 17, 63 percent of the fundamentalists
scored high on media religiosity. When we compare these

patterns with the statistics from conservative and moderate
religious denominations, we observe markable differences
(i.e., lower average scores) in all cases statistically significant. However, although these data help us to see an
emerging "Moral Majority" supporter-type, there must be considered the realistic problem of interactive statistical
effects when attempting to analyze a series of bivariate, or
paired, relationships. Therefore, we conducted multivari-
ate (multiple regression) analysis, estimating the effect
of each independent variable on the dependent variable (support for the Moral Majority) while simultaneously control-
ling for the effects of all other independent variables considered together, not only for the total sample but also
for within each denomination. This final analytical phase
is presented in Table 18.

TABLE 18:   THE EFFECTS OF RELIGIOUS ATTITUDES AND BEHAVIOR
ON SUPPORT FOR THE MORAL MAJORITY EMPLOYING
MULTIPLE REGRESSION ANALYSIS

VARIABLE	TOTAL SAMPLE		FUNDAMENTALIST		CONSERVATIVE		MODER-ATE	
	r	F	r	F	r	B	r	B
Media Reli-giosity	.33	20.29	.53	11.05	.27	.19	.14	.12
Religious Orthodoxy	.32	3.33	.48	5.56	.24	.11	.11	-.04
Civil Re-ligion	.30	6.35	.27	.00	.20	.09	.20	.15
Church Re-ligiosity	.19	.19	.44	3.32	.11	-.02	.01	-.07
Totals	R^2=.206		R^2 =.493		R^2 =.105		R^2=.086	
	R = .44		R = .70		R = .32		R = .29	
	F = 23.11		F = 9.13		F = 3.78		F = 1.64	
	Pr = .001		Pr= .001		Pr= .01		N.S.	

Table 18 removes all doubt in our attempt to clarify just *who* constitutes the grass roots support for the Moral Majority. In multiple regression analysis the computer selects independent variables in their order of explanatory power; clearly media religiosity, followed by religious orthodoxy, has the most importance. Civil religion is a distinct third while church religiosity becomes virtually insignificant. In other words, knowing respondents' frequency of attending to the electronic church, and how conservative is their Christianity, are the two best predictors of whether or not they will support the Moral Majority. Supporters are indisputably more likely to be fundamentalist and conservative Christians.

After separating the sample into the three main denominational categories and performing separate regression analyses within each, we see that the variation in the total sample is largely explained by the fundamentalists. It is *their* media religiosity and religious orthodoxy that make the first two independent variables significantly related to support for the Moral Majority in the larger sample. Indeed, not only are the conservatives' coefficients weaker than the fundamentalists, the moderates' coefficients are statistically insignificant.

Another important finding is that attitudes of civil religion are not nearly as important as one might expect. It seems that when supporters of the Moral Majority "attend" to media religious messages they are more receptive to the religious aspects and less concerned with the civil (i.e., political) aspects. In fact, there is evidence that those in our sample who reported participation in the electronic church (here dealing only with television) did not watch the more politically oriented evangelists. As Table 19 demonstrates, the most frequently viewed religious television programs by our respondents were not ones with a civil religious cr political bent.

TABLE 19: DISTRIBUTION OF RELIGIOUS T.V. VIEWERS

PROGRAM	N	%
Local Church Services	97	21
Billy Graham	80	17
Oral Roberts	69	15
Pat Robertson (700 Club)	64	14
Other Programs	39	8
James Robison	29	6
Robert Schuller	24	5
Rex Humbard	14	3
Miscellaneous Others	13	3
Jimmy Swaggart	12	2
Jim Bakker (PTL)	11	2
Jerry Falwell	9	2
Kenneth Copeland	3	1
Ernest Angley	3	1

TOTAL PROGRAMS WATCHED   467
TOTAL RESPONDENTS   306
MEAN NUMBER OF PROGRAMS WATCHED   1.5

The most frequently viewed programs reported were:
(1) local church services; (2) Billy Graham (who has re-
pudiated the New Religious Right after his own calamitous
experiences with Richard Nixon during the Watergate scan-
dal); (3) Oral Roberts (who refused to become involved in
conservative political affairs); and (4) Pat Robertson's
700 Club (which does contain civil religious messages but
none overtly politically partisan; and (5) "other programs"
(e.g., the Lutherans' "Davey and Goliath"). The politically outspoken pastors ranked poorly. James Robison managed
a sixth place, but he undoubtedly did that well in the ar-
ray because he is a much-publicized "favorite son" among
televangelists in this area of the Bible belt. Virginia-
based Jerry Falwell, who has considerably more national
recognition than Robison, ranked 12th out of 14 types of

programs (only nine persons in our entire sample reported
watching him).

Thus there is considerable reason to doubt that the
politically oriented televangelists have yet mobilized more
than a rather small percentage of the general population.

SUMMARY

The focus of this chapter has been to ask the question of whether the Moral Majority is best regarded as a
political or as a religious movement. Our findings from
the 1981 General Population Survey lead us to conclude that
it is largely a fundamentalist Christian movement and that
a tiny percentage of the general population watches or supports its television ministries.

Moreover, the Moral Majority's supporters differ from
both neutrals and non-supporters in statistically significant ways on a number of dimensions. Supporters show high
agreement with statements expressing civil religious sentiments and are the most likely to agree that religion should
be involved in the political process. At the same time, an
interesting proportion of dissenters (38 percent) within
the supporters subsample *disagrees* that religion should be
involved with politics. Nor did all supporters score high
on the civil religion index. This suggests that evidence
of strong civil religious sentiments does not necessarily
constitute evidence of support for direct political involvement of religion. Conversely, many persons who say they
endorse the Moral Majority movement do not possess strong
civil religious sentiments. This last finding is consistent with our argument that the Moral Majority is disproportionately attractive to fundamentalist Christians and
progressively less so to conservative, moderates, and Catholics because it is essentially a fundamentalist Christian

movement.

The relationships of other variables with support for the Moral Majority were investigated. We discovered significant relationships between support for the Moral Majority and church religiosity, media religiosity, and religious orthodoxy. Supporters of the movement, in other words, are the most likely to be active churchgoers, religious television programming watchers, and literalist in biblical interpretation. Pursuing this logic we probed for the relation between denomination and each of those latter three variables since we had previously found denomination to be significantly associated with support for the Moral Majority. It in turn was significantly related to this support.

Finally, examining through multiple regression analysis the independent estimated relationship of each variable to support for the Moral Majority, media religiosity and religious orthodoxy were found to be the two most important predictors, especially among fundamentalists (less so among conservatives and not at all among moderates). This finding, plus a tally of just what specific religious television programs are viewed by our sample, reinforced the interpretation that viewers are attending more to the religious dimension in civil religion than to the civil dimension.

CHAPTER V

THE MORAL MAJORITY FROM THE
MINORITY VANTAGE POINT

The Moral Majority has claimed to be a multi-racial
political party that provides political support for all ethnic and religious groups and organizations in American society. However, political conservatives have not traditionally received the support of minority groups, and conversely most political party platforms of conservative parties
have not been sympathetic to the needs of minority groups.
In this chapter we examine the minority subsample in our
General Population Survey. While there were only 60 persons in this group, it is nevertheless large enough to form
a preliminary picture of minority support for the Moral Majority and its platform.

MINORITY GROUPS AND POLITICAL
ISSUES OF THE MORAL MAJORITY

According to the 1980 Census, minority groups comprise
approximately 19 percent of the total population of the
United States. Among the minorities the black population
is the largest numerical minority with 11.7 percent or

26,910,000 people. The Hispanic population represents approximately 6.4 percent of the total population or
14,720,000 persons. The remainder of the minority population consists of Orientals, American Indians and others.
Furthermore, there are 3,100 counties in the United States,
103 counties have black populations of at least 50 percent, and these counties are located in the south, the logical stronghold of the Moral Majority.

In recent years, especially since the passage of the
voting rights act which eliminated the poll tax, an increasing number of blacks and Hispanics are registering
and taking an active part in the political process. Recent evidence of political support for minorities becoming
more active in the political process is the television interview of the Governor of Texas (Bill Clements) on January
22, 1982 when he stated that he was a strong supporter of
the Voting Rights Act and plans to testify later this year
in Washington, D.C.

As early as 1970 the Bureau of Census reported that
58 percent of eligible black voters were registered and that
37 percent participated in the political process. If these
proportions have remained constant we are referring to five
and one-half million voters among the black population a-
lone. Thus we feel it is important to discuss how the minorities view the political platform of the Moral Majority.
The data presented in Table 20 show the frequency distribution of ethnic groups on the key political issues supported by the leadership of the Moral Majority.

TABLE 20:   BASIC ISSUES OF THE MORAL MAJORITY AMONG
                            MINORITIES

ISSUES	BLACK		MEXICAN-AMERICAN		OTHER	
	N	%	N	%	N	%
1. Abortion is a sin against God's law.						
Agree	11	85	14	78	11	61
Disagree	2	15	4	22	7	39
2. I believe in the ERA to guarantee women equal rights.						
Agree	16	100	13	68	11	65
Disagree	0	0	6	6	36	35
3. Evolution should be taught in school.						
Agree	12	75	14	82	11	65
Disagree	4	25	3	18	6	35
4. The biblical account of creation should be taught in school.						
Agree	11	92	12	67	12	75
Disagree	1	8	6	33	4	25
5. I think prayer should be allowed in the schools.						
Agree	16	100	13	68	15	83
Disagree	0	0	6	32	3	17
6. Sex education should be taught in the schools.						
Agree	16	100	14	74	13	72
Disagree	0	0	5	26	5	28

Our data reveal a very conservative sample of minority respondents. In fact, our minority sample is much more
supportive on some of the basic political issues of the

Moral Majority than our sample of white respondents. For
example; on abortion, evolution, and creation theory, the
minorities are much more supportive than the white sample.
There is practically no difference between the minorities
and the white respondents on the issue involving prayer in
school. However, we did find that the minorities were significantly higher in their support for the Equal Rights
Amendment and sex education being taught in the public
school system.

Perhaps we should point out again that our sample data are predominately middle-class home-owning respondents
with about 90 percent participating in the 1980 elections.
Since home-owning and high rates of voting are characteristics generally true for the entire sample we can conclude
that minorities who have achieved middle-class status in
American society tend to reflect what they perceive as middle-class values. In other words, on some of the key Moral Majority issues, minorities tend to be super moralists,
perhaps out of a "cult of gratitude". We feel this conclusion is verified by the high percentage of respondents who
are opposed to legalized abortion, who feel that creation
theory should be a part of the school content curriculum,
and who feel that prayer should be allowed in school. All
of these issues reflect basic Christian values which are
traditionally supported by the larger white middle-class.

On the other hand, when we focus on issues that reflect attitudes and behaviors grounded in prejudice and
discrimination, we find the minorities are understandably
more supportive of these political issues than the white
respondents. For example, they are much more likely to support the Equal Rights Amendment. Minority groups have experienced the effects of discrimination and likely believe
that it is only through the legislative acts of Congress
that equal treatment can be achieved. Thus we find that

100 percent of the black respondents are supportive of the
Equal Rights Amendment. Among the Mexican-Americans and
other minority groups the proportion supporting the Equal
Rights Amendment is approximately the same as we find among
the white respondents. Data presented in Table 21 compares
white respondents with all minority respondents on the basic issues.

TABLE 21:   COMPARISON OF WHITE AND MINORITIES ON THE BASIC
            POLITICAL ISSUES OF THE MORAL MAJORITY

ISSUES	WHITE		MINORITIES	
	N	%	N	%
1. Abortion				
Agree	341	52	36	73
Disagree	316	48	13	27
2. ERA				
Agree	452	67	40	77
Disagree	226	33	12	23
3. Evolution				
Agree	418	62	37	74
Disagree	252	38	13	26
4. Creation				
Agree	461	73	35	76
Disagree	170	27	11	24
5. Prayer				
Agree	600	87	44	83
Disagree	88	13	9	17
6. Sex Educ.				
Agree	549	81	43	81
Disagree	131	19	10	19

These data show there is a high degree of consensus
among members of minority groups and the white respondents
though there is a tendency for the former to be more conservative on three issues. The only issue in which there is

a statistically significant difference concerns the issue
on abortion. The minorities are much more conservative
with 73 percent agreeing that "Abortion is a sin against
God's law" compared to 52 percent of the white respondents.
Thus we conclude that minorities either resemble their white
counterparts or at times demonstrate more conservative positions on the basic political issues of the Moral Majority.

CIVIL RELIGION, MEDIA RELIGIOSITY, CHURCH RELIGIOSITY,
AND CHRISTIAN ORTHODOXY AMONG THE MINORITY GROUPS

In our previous discussion of this study's four main
indices we presented evidence of the interrelatedness of
these measures and support for the Moral Majority among the
white respondents. Here, we present a comparison of how
the minorities feel about these selected, and highly relevant attitudes and opinions with whites. The data presented in Table 22 presents our findings.

TABLE 22: COMPARATIVE ANALYSIS OF WHITE AND MINORITY RE-
SPONDENTS ON SELECTED INDICES

	CIVIL RELIGION			
	WHITE		MINORITIES	
	N	%	N	%
Low	232	33	16	30
Medium	327	46	25	47
High	152	21	12	23

	MEDIA RELIGIOSITY			
	WHITE		MINORITIES	
	N	%	N	%
Low	471	66	37	70
Medium	126	18	10	19
High	114	16	6	11

TABLE 22: COMPARATIVE ANALYSIS OF WHITE AND MINORITY
           RESPONDENTS ON SELECTED INDICES (CONT.)

CHURCH RELIGIOSITY

	WHITE		MINORITIES	
	N	%	N	%
Low	151	21	10	19
High	560	79	43	81

CHRISTIAN ORTHODOXY

	WHITE		MINORITIES	
	N	%	N	%
Low	144	20	7	13
Medium	195	28	19	36
High	372	52	27	51

Our data show quite clearly that there is no significant difference between minority groups and white respondents on indicators of civil religion, media religiosity,
church religiosity and Christian orthodoxy.

In sum, up to this point in the analysis we have demonstrated that the minorities in our sample are very similar to the white respondents on the selected political issues of the Moral Majority and behavioral and attitudinal
indices that related to support for the Moral Majority.

RELIGIOUS DENOMINATION AND ETHNICITY

Among the white respondents we found that denomination was an important factor in identifying supporters of
the Moral Majority. Therefore we included denomination of
the ethnic subsample. For comparative purposes the white
respondents were included. Table 23 presents our findings.

TABLE 23:   THE RELATIONSHIP BETWEEN ETHNICITY AND
                        DENOMINATION

DENOMINATION	WHITE		MINORITIES	
	N	%	N	%
Fundamental	75	13	10	21
Conservative	238	42	14	29
Moderate	164	29	4	8
Catholic	90	16	20	42
Total	567	100.0	48	100.0

$x^2 = 27.0$ Pr. $= .001$ V $= .21$

Table 23 demonstrates a statistically significant relationship between ethnicity and religious denomination.
The relationship can be explained by the fact that we have
a higher proportion of fundamentalists and Catholics among
the minority groups. Among the minorities 21 percent are
fundamentalists compared to only 13 percent of the white
respondents. Forty-two percent of the minority groups
are Catholic compared to only 16 percent of the white respondents. Only 8 percent of the minorities are classified
in moderate religious denominations.

The religious conservativism among the minority groups
logically might lead us to assume that we may find them to
be quite supportive of the Moral Majority as a social movement. The final section allows us to test this hypothesis.

MINORITY GROUPS AND SUPPORT FOR
THE MORAL MAJORITY

In our final analysis of the minority subsample we are interested in gauging their support for the Moral Majority. We found that among the white respondents that most of the support for the Moral Majority was derived from the fundamentalist religious denominations. The data presented in Table 24 identifies the extent to which the leadership of the Moral Majority can anticipate the support of middle-class minority group members.

TABLE 24: THE RELATIONSHIP BETWEEN ETHNICITY AND SUPPORT
FOR THE MORAL MAJORITY

	WHITE		MINORITIES	
	N	%	N	%
Supporters	111	16	2	4
Indifferent	379	53	39	74
Non-Supporters	220	31	12	22
Total	710	100.0	53	100.0

x^2 = 9.5   Pr. = .008   V = .11

There is a statistically significant relationship between ethnicity and support for the Moral Majority. Only 4 percent of the minority respondents (1 black and 1 oriental) indicate support for the movement. This finding may seem to contradict what we have seen thus far. That is, we have already noted that minorities are more in agreement with the Moral Majority in terms of specific issues than are the white respondents, yet only 2 members of our minority subsample support the Moral Majority. There are 6

times as many persons who reject it. Almost three-fourths
are indifferent to it.

The implications are obvious. In our Texas sample,
which we believe has critical implications for the New
Religious Right not only in the Bible belt but elsewhere in
the nation, the Moral Majority is appealing primarily to
white, Anglo Americans. Furthermore, the dynamics of the
main avenue of appeal for whites -- denomination -- does
not operate in the same way for minorities. In particular,
the Hispanics' tendency to be Roman Catholic, and the lack
of Roman Catholic leadership in the Moral Majority, means
that within that subsample religious orthodoxy does not
guarantee attraction to the Moral Majority's conservative
religious flavor.

SUMMARY

The minority subsample resembles the larger white subsample on most measures, with a slight tendency to be more
conservative on issues such as abortion and prayer in
schools. Minority respondents also are predominantly in denominations with traditional religious orthodoxy (fundamentalist, conservative, and Roman Catholic). Yet we observed
only a trace of support for the Moral Majority. The majority of our minority subsample is indifferent to the movement, with non-support proportionately greater than among
white Anglos. Earlier we concluded that the Moral Majority
is largely a fundamentalist Christian movement. Here we
must qualify that conclusion and note its ethnic/racial
homogeneity as well.

CHAPTER VI

PERSPECTIVES OF THE CLERGY TOWARD
THE MORAL MAJORITY

Estimating that there are roughly 350,000 to 400,000
ministers currently in the United States, Jerry Falwell
(1981c) criticized them for their failure to preach against
the immoralities of modern America:

> There are many who do keep their silence in the
> pulpit, and I am afraid that's the reason, the
> primary reason, our country is in the spiritual
> condition it's in today. . . . I'm convinced if
> a hundred thousand pastors in America would get
> the message from God and begin preaching it
> fearlessly we could change our society quickly.
> . . . Many of our churches are nothing but re-
> ligious country clubs, social mortuaries. And
> we need to put a wreath out on the door, or
> start preaching the truth, one of the two.

The Reverend Greg Dixon, National Secretary of the
Moral Majority, Inc., has put the failings of many liberal
and mainline ministers in even blunter words. Terming the
National Council of Churches a group whose goals parallel
the communist party and its president, United Methodist

Bishop James Armstrong, a socialist, he stated:
>   There is no question in my mind that Communists
>   are in many of the pulpits of the old-line de-
>   nominations across America -- who are not Chris-
>   tians at all. They are wolves in sheep's cloth-
>   ing. (*Dallas Morning News*, January 23, 1982).

Falwell believes that the clergy can and must lead to
a reversal in the moral direction of this nation. Indeed,
with that state of mind they could eliminate such problems as
pornography and abortion. On the last problem he predicted:
>   The time needs to come in this nation when
>   the preachers so take their stand, not con-
>   trolling the country but providing a con-
>   science for the country, that you cannot
>   be elected to any governing position, any
>   elective office, at any level unless you
>   are willing to live and die for the pro-
>   tection of the human and civil rights of
>   unborn babies.

But are America's preachers "silent" on certain issues
of concern to Falwell out of lack of courage or conviction,
as Falwell has repeatedly implied in sermons on the *Old Time
Gospel Hour* program? Do they agree with his view of *the*
Christian response to these issues and of their own alleged
left-wing tendencies? Do they sympathize with Falwell's
campaign to return (or at least introduce) morality to politics?

THE CLERGY AND THE MORAL MAJORITY

Until this survey the only view of the clergy towards
the Moral Majority and its political platform systematically
presented were those of the spokespersons of "televangelical"
ministry. The average citizen could easily conclude that

Falwell, Robison, and a few other "televangelists" represented the religious and political perspectives of most
clergy in the absence of reliable research. Our 1981 Ministerial Survey of clergymen's attitudes was designed to
accomplish three basic objectives: (1) to determine how
the clergy feels towards the basic political issues being
addressed by the Moral Majority; (2) to determine the extent to which the Moral Majority reflects the views of the
clergy; and (3) to compare the clergy by denomination on
these issues. Here we focus on these three questions. In
Chapter Seven we will examine the clergy's sentiments about
religion's involvement in politics and compare them to the
general population.

THE CLERGY AND THE BASIC POLITICAL
PLATFORM OF THE MORAL MAJORITY

One of the major goals of the Moral Majority is to involve ministers in the political processes of this country.
As we noted in Chapter Four, evangelist James Robison stated
in a newspaper interview that he intended to take 1,000
preachers to Washington and teach them the art of politics.
The logical assumption underlying such a claim would be that
there are in fact, in this Bible-belt region, 1,000 ministers who subscribe to the basic philosophy of the Moral Majority. We included in our survey questions probing attitudes of the clergy toward the legislative amendments central to the political goals of the Moral Majority in order
to gauge the potential of a clerical support base for the
Moral Majority. The data contained in Table 25 represent
the attitudes of all clergy in our sample toward these proposed legislative activities.[1]

TABLE 25:   FREQUENCY DISTRIBUTION OF CLERGY'S RESPONSE TO
                    POLITICAL ISSUES

ITEM	N	%
1. Amend Constitution to prohibit abortion		
Agree	82	53
Disagree	63	41
No Response	9	6
Total	154	100.0
2. Amend Constitution to guarantee ÉRA		
Agree	82	53
Disagree	63	41
No Response	9	6
Total	154	100.0
3. Amend Constitution to permit prayer in school		
Agree	83	54
Disagree	66	43
No Response	5	3
Total	154	100.0
4. Amend constitution to mandate creation theory be taught along with evolutionary theory		
Agree	83	54
Disagree	66	43
No Response	4	3
Total	154	100.0
5. Amend Constitution giving equal rights to homosexuals		
Agree	41	27
Disagree	106	69
No Response	7	4
Total	154	100.0
6. Need more legislation to control pornography		
Agree	115	75
Disagree	35	23
No Response	4	2
Total	154	100.0

The data presented above represent the views of the
clergy on the six frequently cited concerns of the Moral
Majority. At the time of this writing the Moral Majority
was employing lobbying pressure to obtain enough votes in
the House of Representatives to pass the Pro-Life (Anti-
Abortion) Amendment. This amendment would make abortion
illegal under almost every circumstance including rape and
when the mother's life is in danger. Among the Dallas-
Fort Worth clergy whom we sampled, 82 (53 percent) indicate
that they agree with the Moral Majority on this issue.

A second political issue that has been especially
relevant at this time concerns the attitudes of the clergy
on the Equal Rights Amendment for women. Among the pri-
mary goals of the Moral Majority is the defeat of the Equal
Rights Amendment. The leadership of the entire New Religious Right favor the traditional role of women and feel
that passage of the Equal Rights Amendment will contribute
to the deterioration of the family in American society. In
our sample of Texas clergymen we found considerable disagreement: as on the first issue, respondents are nearly
evenly split. Fifty-three percent of the ministers favor
passage of the Equal Rights Amendment.

A third political issue that has been debated since
the O'Hare decision in the early 1960's pertains to prayer
in school. According to the Moral Majority and their anti-
secular orientation, secular humanists are responsible for
much of the apathy and hedonistic attitude and behavior of
American youth. The proponents of the Moral Majority frequently indicate that prayer in schools would help point the
youth of today in the "right" direction. Slightly over one-
half (54 percent) of our sample agree that prayer should be
a part of the school curriculum.

A fourth political issue that has recently received
nationwide attention is the 1981-82 court trial in the

state of Arkansas involving the constitutionality of a
state law requiring the teaching of creation theory if evolutionary theory is also taught in the public schools. Numerous statements have been made by New Religious Right
leaders advocating the teaching of creation theory in the
public school as a viable alternative to evolutionary
theory. In this trial the judge eventually ruled against
the state of Arkansas and in his conclusion stated that
creation theory is not a scientific theory (but rather an
attempt to promote the biblical account of divine creation) and therefore was not admissible as an alternative to
evolutionary theory. Since the data analyzed in our research were collected some months prior to this trial and
decision, we do not feel that our data were contaminated by
this ruling. Our results show that 54 percent of the clergy feel that creation theory should be a part of the public
school curriculum.

Two other issues are considered important to the pro-
family political perspective of the Moral Majority. These
issues involve equal rights for homosexuals and more legal
control of pornography. Here the ministers approach a consensus more than on the previous four issues. Our data show
that most clergy (69 percent) are opposed to equal rights
for homosexuals and that 75 percent agree that we should
have more legal control over pornography.

Nevertheless, the frequency distributions of the clergy sample clearly indicate that the leadership of the Moral Majority does not reflect a consensually supported platform of issues. The clergy themselves are decidedly split
on the moral status of such issues as abortion, prayer in
schools, creation theory, and the passage of the Equal
Rights Amendment.

SUPPORT FOR THE MORAL MAJORITY AND THE
POLITICAL ISSUES AMONG THE CLERGY

The preceding discussion elaborated the dispersion a-
mong the ministry on the key political concerns of the Moral Majority. The sample clergy were also asked, "How do
you feel about the Moral Majority?" similar to the question asked of the general population (see Chapter Three).
Their responses allowed us to classify the ministers into
three categories: supporters of the Moral Majority, those
indifferent or apathetic toward the Moral Majority, and
clergy who are definitely opposed or non-supportive of the
Moral Majority. By classifying the ministers into these
three categories it was possible to test statistically the
relationship between support for the Moral Majority and
the attitudes of the clergy towards basic political issues.

SUPPORT FOR THE MORAL MAJORITY AND
ATTITUDES TOWARD ABORTION

Frequently, in the political arena the terminology
used to describe the parameters of an issue is extremely re-
vealing. For example, the word "abortion" has very negative
connotations whereas use of the concept "pro-life" and "pro-
choice" tend to evoke somewhat different responses. (It becomes then possible to point to those on the opposite side
of the issue as "anti-life" and "anti-choice"). We asked
the clergy, "would you favor a constitutional amendment
that prohibits abortion?" We predicted that a significantly high proportion of the supporters of the Moral Majority
would favor a constitutional amendment prohibiting abortion.
The results are presented in Table 26.

TABLE 26:   THE RELATIONSHIP BETWEEN SUPPORT FOR THE MORAL
             MAJORITY AND ATTITUDES TOWARD ABORTION
             AMONG THE CLERGY

ABORTION	SUPPORT		INDIFFERENT		NON-SUPPORTERS	
	N	%	N	%	N	%
Agree	32	91	30	63	19	30
Disagree	3	9	18	37	45	70
Total	35	100.0	48	100.0	64	100.0

$x^2 = 36.4$ Pr. $= .0001$ V $= .50$

The hypothesized relationship between support for the
Moral Majority and attitudes toward legislation to prohibit
abortion is supported by the data. Among the supporters
of the Moral Majority, we find that 91 percent or 32 of the
35 clergymen identified as supporters of the Moral Majority
agree that legislation is needed to prohibit abortion.
When we focus on ministers who are opposed to the Moral Majority we find that 45 or 70 percent are opposed to this
type legislation.

SUPPORT FOR THE MORAL MAJORITY AND

THE EQUAL RIGHTS AMENDMENT

To reiterate, New Religious Right spokespersons such
as Jerry Falwell and James Robison have presented a pro-
family perspective integral to the platform of the Moral
Majority. They assume that the passage of the Equal Rights
Amendment would destroy the traditional family institution
in American society. We predicted that ministers supporting the platform of the Moral Majority would be against an
amendment that would guarantee equal rights for women,

perceiving it as a potential threat to traditional family
patterns via its purported purpose to remove women from
their domestic functions. The data presented in Table 27
support our position.

TABLE 27: THE RELATIONSHIP BETWEEN SUPPORT FOR THE MORAL
MAJORITY AND ATTITUDES TOWARD E.R.A. AMONG THE
CLERGY

	SUPPORT		INDIFFERENT		NON-SUPPORTERS	
	N	%	N	%	N	%
Favor	7	21	24	52	49	77
Oppose	26	79	22	48	15	23
Total	33	100.0	46	100.0	64	100.0

x^2 = 27.5   Pr = .0001   V = .44

Although the data are quite conclusive, with 79 percent of the supporters of the Moral Majority opposed to
the Equal Rights Amendment while 77 percent of the non-supporters favor the amendment, it is interesting to note that
there is some disagreement among the supporters. As noted
in Table 27, over 20 percent of the supporters of the Moral
Majority favor the amendment. And, as noted in Table 25 a
majority of most clergy support the Equal Rights Amendment.
Thus, based on our data, we can conclude that all clergy
are (understandably) pro-family but that a majority do not
feel that the guarantee of equal rights for women will significantly affect the family orientation and structure in
American society.

SUPPORT FOR THE MORAL MAJORITY

AND PRAYER IN SCHOOL

In 1948 the Supreme Court ruled that the use of public schools for the purpose of religious instruction vio-
lated the First and Fourteenth Amendments. In 1962, after
several citizens in New York brought action against the Re-
gents for instituting a particular prayer at the beginning
of each school day, the Supreme Court ruled that this vio-
lated the separation of church and state doctrine. However
there have been continuing efforts by lay persons as well
as ministers to reinstate the custom of prayer in the public
school system. Until recently the separation of church and
state doctrine has been upheld by the states and independent
school districts within the municipalities. However, within the past year there has been a resurrection of efforts
to include prayer in the public school curriculum. The
data contained in Table 28 analyze how the clergy feel about
prayer in school.

TABLE 28: THE RELATIONSHIP BETWEEN SUPPORT FOR THE MORAL
           MAJORITY AND ATTITUDES TOWARD PRAYER IN SCHOOL

PRAYER	SUPPORT		INDIFFERENT		NON-SUPPORTERS	
	N	%	N	%	N	%
Favor	30	88	33	67	18	28
Oppose	4	12	16	33	46	72
Total	34	100.0	49	100.0	64	100.0

$x^2 = 36.9$ Pr. = .0001   V = .50

The hypothesized relationship between support for the
Moral Majority and amending the constitution to allow prayer
in school is statistically significant. Among the Moral

Majority supporters 88 percent of the clergy favor an
amendment while only 28 percent of the non-supporters
favor such an amendment. Overall, 43 percent of the clergy
are opposed to prayer in school.

SUPPORT FOR THE MORAL MAJORITY
AND CREATION THEORY

Another basic concern of the Moral Majority is the
teaching of evolutionary theory as a scientific fact and
the absense of creation theory as an alternative theory.
This issue, thought many Americans, was laid to rest after
the notorious 1920's "Scopes" monkey trial. However, evolutionary theory's domination in biology and science class-
rooms was recently challenged in the Federal District Court
in Arkansas. On January 5, 1982 the judge rendered his conclusion that the state had not provided sufficient evidence
to justify the inclusion of the biblical account of creation
into the public school curriculum. We hypothesized that a-
among the clergy, supporters of the political platform of the
Moral Majority would endorse creation theory as a mandate
for the public school curriculum. Our findings are presented in Table 29.

TABLE 29: THE RELATIONSHIP BETWEEN SUPPORT FOR THE MORAL
MAJORITY AND ATTITUDES TOWARD TEACHING CREATION
THEORY IN SCHOOL

CREATION THEORY	SUPPORT		INDIFFERENT		NON-SUPPORTERS	
	N	%	N	%	N	%
Favor	31	91	37	76	14	21
Oppose	3	9	12	24	51	79
Total	34	100.0	49	100.0	65	100.0

$x^2 = 55.8$ Pr. = .0001   V = 0.61

There is a very strong and statistically significant
relationship between support for the Moral Majority and attitudes towards teaching creation theory in the public
schools. Among the clergy supporting the Moral Majority 91
percent approve of legislation mandating the teaching of
creation theory as an alternative theory compared to only
21 percent of the non-supporters.

SUPPORT FOR THE MORAL MAJORITY AND PORNOGRAPHY

For decades there has been debate over the definition
of what constitutes pornographic material and who should
have access to such material. We are constantly reminded
in the popular media (press and video) of the dangers of ex-
posure to violence, human sexuality, and obscene language.
Numerous groups are presently involved in censoring movies,
television programming, and textbooks utilized in the public
school system. Based on the tremendous amount of activity
concerned with pornographic materials we predicted that supporters of the Moral Majority would favor more control over
pornography. Our findings are presented in Table 30.

TABLE 30:   THE RELATIONSHIP BETWEEN SUPPORT FOR THE MORAL
            MAJORITY AND ATTITUDES TOWARD PORNOGRAPHY
            AMONG THE CLERGY

PORNOGRAPHY	SUPPORT		INDIFFERENT		NON-SUPPORTERS	
	N	%	N	%	N	%
Favor More Con-trol	32	94	41	84	41	63
Don't Favor More Control	2	6	8	16	24	37
Total	34	100.0	49	100.0	65	100.0

$x^2 = 14.0$ Pr. = .0009   V = .31

As anticipated, we find that a majority of the clergy
do support legislation that would result in more control
over pornography in American society. And, the supporters
of the Moral Majority feel much stronger about this specific issue than the non-supporters with 94 percent of the
supporters reflecting attitudes similar to those perspectives advocated by the Moral Majority.

SUPPORT FOR THE MORAL MAJORITY
AND EQUAL RIGHTS FOR HOMOSEXUALS

An issue that has received national attention for the
past decade has been the gay rights liberation movement.
Numerous demonstrations and several court decisions have
been rendered that have provided some protection for persons whose sexual preference does not follow the traditional heterosexual pattern. The leaders of the Moral Majority
have expressed the view that homosexuality is a sin against
God and is disruptive to the traditional family orientation. In 1979 the local representative of the New Religious Right, James Robison, had his religious program on
one of the major television channels discontinued by the
network because of allegedly derogatory remarks made during
one of his sermons regarding homosexuals. Since this is
an important and controversial issue we included in our survey the opinions of the clergy towards equal rights of persons regardless of sexual preference. Table 31 contains our
findings.

TABLE 31: THE RELATIONSHIP BETWEEN SUPPORT FOR THE MORAL
MAJORITY AND ATTITUDES TOWARD RIGHTS FOR
HOMOSEXUALS

HOMOSEXUALS	SUPPORT		INDIFFERENT		NON-SUPPORTERS	
	N	%	N	%	N	%
Favor	4	11	8	16	28	46
Oppose	31	89	41	84	33	54
Total	35	100.0	49	100.0	61	100.0

$x^2 = 17.9$ Pr. = .0001   V = .35

First, an overwhelming majority of the clergy are
opposed to legislation providing equal rights for homosexuals (74 percent). However, we did obtain a statistically
significant relationship between support for the Moral Majority and equal rights for homosexuals with 89 percent
of the supporters opposed compared to 54 percent of the non-
supporters. Homosexuals find few sympathizers in this sample, but they discover fewest among supporters of the Moral
Majority.

THE DENOMINATIONAL DETERMINANT

In previous analysis of support for the Moral Majority
on key political issues we found that denomination is an
aspect that must be taken into consideration in understanding the origins of the attitudes and opinions regarding the
Moral Majority. The clergy were classified into four categories. This classification includes fundamentalists, conservatives, moderate ministers and Catholic priests. Table
32 summarizes the relationships between denomination of the
clergy and support on key political issues.

TABLE 32: SUMMARY TABLE OF RELATIONSHIP BETWEEN RELIGIOUS
DENOMINATION AND KEY POLITICAL ISSUES USING CHI-
SQUARE DISTRIBUTIONS

$X_1 = 25.7$	$X_3 = 16.9$	$X_5 = 11.2$
$V_1 = .42$	$V_3 = .34$	$V_5 = .28$
$X_2 = 17.6$	$X_4 = 21.7$	$X_6 = 25.8$
$V_2 = .35$	$V_4 = .39$	$V_6 = .42$

All relationships are statistically significant

*See Tables 34-39 in Appendix A

X_1 = Relationship between denomination and abortion
X_2 = Relationship between denomination and ERA
X_3 = Relationship between denomination and Prayer
X_4 = Relationship between denomination and Creation Theory
X_5 = Relationship between denomination and Pornography
X_6 = Relationship between denomination and Homosexuality

In summarizing the data concerning the relationships
between denominations and support for the key platform issues of the Moral Majority we obtained the following information: (1) 76 percent of the fundamentalists support legislation prohibiting abortion compared to 25 percent of the
moderates; (2) approximately 52 percent of the fundamentalists are opposed to equal rights for women compared to 14
percent of the moderates; (3) 75 percent of the fundamentalists favor prayer in school compared to 44 percent of
the moderates; (4) 81 percent of the fundamentalists support the teaching of creation theory compared to almost 29
percent of the moderates; (5) 92 percent of the fundamentalists are in favor of more legislative control over pornography compared to almost 63 percent of moderates; (6) 95
percent of the fundamentalists are opposed to equal rights
for homosexuals compared to 44 percent of the moderates.
The Catholic priests were distributed in the following man-
ner: (1) 90 percent oppose abortion (2) 67 percent support

ERA; (3) 90 percent favor prayer in school; (4) 44 percent
favor creation theory; (5) 60 percent favor more control
over pornography; and (6) 50 percent support equal rights
for homosexuals.

Finally, the findings concerning the relationship between denomination of the clergy and support for key issues
of the political platform of the Moral Majority are illumi-
nated in the following section.

DENOMINATION AND SUPPORT FOR THE MORAL MAJORITY

In our analysis of the clergy and the extent to which
they are supportive of the political platform of the Moral
Majority we have found that how the clergy feels about the
Moral Majority as a political party and the denomination of
the clergy are two highly important factors that must be
considered in understanding the dynamics of the support for
the Moral Majority and the extent of support. The following data in Table 33 permit us to elaborate on these factors.

TABLE 33:   THE RELATIONSHIP BETWEEN SUPPORT FOR THE MORAL
            MAJORITY AND DENOMINATION AMONG THE CLERGY

MORAL MAJ.	FUNDAMENTAL		CONSERVATIVE		MODERATES		CATHOLIC	
	N	%	N	%	N	%	N	%
Supporters	16	38	14	23	2	5	3	33
Indifferent	17	41	20	33	8	22	3	33
Non-Support-ers	9	21	26	44	27	73	3	34
Total	42	100.0	60	100.0	37	100.0	9	100.0

$x^2 = 23.6$ Pr. = .0006   V = .28

This data show quite conclusively that support for the

Moral Majority tends to be found among the fundamentalists, with 38 percent indicating that they support the movement. Only 23 percent of the clergy in the conservative denominations are supportive. When we focus on clergy representing moderate denominations, a mere 5 percent indicate they are supportive of the Moral Majority. Catholics are evenly divided on the 3 postures (3 in favor of each). It is not clear if a larger sampling of the latter would produce the same distribution.

SUMMARY

The clergy represent a heterogeneous group with regard to their opinions on key social issues and their feelings of support toward the Moral Majority. Consistently, we have seen fundamentalists take extremely conservative views on social issues with moderates taking more liberal positions and the conservatives in-between. Likewise, fundamentalists are more likely to support the Moral Majority, moderates are least likely, and conservatives are in the middle. Quite clearly, support for the Moral Majority is a good predictor of positions on the six social issues discussed here, and in turn a clergyman's denomination is the best predictor of that support as well as positions on those social issues. The latter finding concerning denomination's determining influence on individual clergymen's attitudes regarding social issues is consistent with previous research when clergy were concerned with a different set of social issues (e.g., Shupe and Wood, 1973).

In short, clergymen's responses to the questions about the Moral Majority and various social issues are best predicted, or explained, by knowing their specific denominations. The Moral Majority, it would seem, is not an interdenominational movement if we speak in terms of denominational proportions.

CHAPTER SIX FOOTNOTES

[1]Respondents were read the following statement before
presenting the various issues: "The Moral Majority has
identified several key issues they feel affect family life
and morality in our society. They feel that it is necessary to use the political arena for legislative purposes.
The following represent the issues. I will read each one
and would appreciate you telling me how you feel about the
issue."

CHAPTER VII

A CRITICAL VIEW OF POPULAR SUPPORT
FOR THE NEW RELIGIOUS RIGHT

Both the 1981 General Population Survey and the 1981
Ministerial Survey in the Bible-belt location of the Dallas-
Fort Worth Metroplex has yielded a number of findings dis-
crepant with the claims of New Religious Right leaders such
as Jerry Falwell, James Robison, and Donald E. Wildmon. Before presenting a critical discussion of the meaning of the
New Religious Right in light of these findings, we briefly
summarize them.

First and foremost at odds with the Moral Majority's
own assertions of its mass popularity, we found no evidence
of any sizeable or "majority" popular support base among
home-owning voters. Far from popular support, we found
twice as many persons opposed to the Moral Majority as for
it, and the largest percentage of our sample either was
made up of persons indifferent towards it or who had never
heard of it. Jerry Falwell once ironically and unwittingly
summed up his true popular influence insofar as our Texas
sample is concerned:

> To suggest that I am a modern-day Pavlov who,
> upon ringing my bell, causes millions of

Americans to salivate to whatever political
tune I am playing is as illogical as it is
ludicrous (Falwell, 1981a: 17).

Since spring, 1981 when the General Population Survey
was conducted, a number of public opinion polls and ex-
perts have presented evidence and views to corroborate our
findings. Aside from those we discussed in Chapter One, a
Washington Post-ABC News national poll of 1,533 persons
found that fully half the sample had never heard of the
Moral Majority. Only one in five of those persons who
could identify it wanted the Moral Majority to exert more
influence in American life while more than 50 percent
thought its influence should be reduced (Peterson and Sussman, 1980). About the same time a Gallup poll found only
40 percent of 1,551 nationally sampled respondents had ever
heard or read of the Moral Majority and only 26 percent
were familiar with its goals and objectives. Those who dis-
approved of the organization outnumbered supporters by 13
to 8 percent (Gallup, 1981). If anything, what these polls
suggest is that our southern Bible-belt sample *overestimated*
the national level of popular support for the Moral Majority in particular and the New Religious Right more generally. Southern Baptist leader James Dunn, chairman of the
Baptist Joint Committee on Public Affairs, concurred:

Their numbers were magnified beyond their impact on the political process, therefore they
have had more influence than they deserve. I
am beginning to sense they do not dominate the
White House (Parmley and Attlesey, 1981).

A second important general conclusion from the 1981
General Population Survey was the divisiveness and inconsistencies of respondents who identified themselves as
Moral Majority supporters across a range of issues such as
abortion, prayer in schools, sex education in schools, and

the influence of so-called secular humanism on youth and
society. The supporters were either surprisingly unin-
formed about the platform of the Moral Majority (calling
their value as supporters into question) or only partially
supportive. We believe the latter to be the case and will
return to its significance shortly as really an issue of
a false consensus claimed for a diverse set of single-
issue groups.

A third important conclusion that can be drawn from
Chapters Three and Four in particular is the essentially
sectarian Christian character of the Moral Majority's supporters. Not all fundamentalists and conservatives supported it, to be sure, but its supporters were most likely to
be fundamentalists and evangelicals and least likely to be
in moderate-to-liberal Protestant denominations. They were
least likely to be Roman Catholics. Thus, Falwell's claims
to possess the loyalty and backing of persons across a
broad panorama of religious groups aside, his support base
seems actually composed of a rather narrow segment of Christians. These are persons high in traditional Christian orthodoxy, active church-goers, and frequent consumers of the
electronic church. However, the bulk of their religious
television consumption is not oriented toward the strong
civil religious and politically oriented messages of Falwell
and his Texas counterpart, James Robison. They appear to
be more interested in the religious, rather than the civil,
dimension in the civil religion messages they are receiving.

A fourth general conclusion concerns the overall negative response to the Moral Majority by minority members
of our general survey sample. Considering their not inconsiderable percentage of the population in this region of
the United States and that the Moral Majority *via* its links
to the electronic church appears to be a southern phenomenon, a further qualification we can make about the Moral

Majority is that it is largely a *white, Anglo* fundamentalist Christian movement. This conclusion was particularly
driven home by the fact that even the fundamentalists in
our minority subsample, who resembled their white, non-minority fundamentalist counterparts on other dimensions such
as religious orthodoxy and on most social issues, failed to
support the Moral Majority.

A fifth general conclusion concerns the divided support of clergymen for the Moral Majority. That support (or
lack of) followed along denominational lines. Fundamentalist clergy were most likely to take stances on controversial proposed constitutional amendments relevant to abortion
the Equal Rights Amendment, and other issues that agree
with the Moral Majority platform, conservative clergy were
less likely, and moderate clergy least likely. Likewise,
supporters of the Moral Majority were most likely to be
fundamentalists, with conservatives and moderates progressively less so. These findings recapitulate the pattern in
our general sample of lay persons. Support for the Moral
Majority is a good predictor of how persons feel about various social issues, and religious denomination is the best
predictor of such support.

BORN AGAIN POLITICS IN RETROSPECT

Jerry Falwell and others have been able, with great
zeal, to create for politicians, journalists, and many citizens an image of the New Religious Right movement as possessing a much larger constituency than it can actually mobilize. This is in large part attributable to astute, aggressive fund-raising techniques that in turn have enabled
certain persons to purchase both electronic media airtime
and the first-class video technology used by them so effec-
tively. However, in the end it is really a case of media

"hype" and good public relations plus wishful thinking on the parts of these persons. When one goes into the actual world seeking honestly and sincerely to find the purported masses of New Religious Right supporters, they are not readily found.

This is certainly not the first time a social movement has been able -- for a time -- to create an image of possessing grossly exaggerated membership size. The Unification Church of America, for example, was able during the 1970's to lend its claims of possessing tens of thousands of members (or "Moonies") through systematic public relations efforts and intensive use of its modest 2,000-3,000 followers (see Bromley and Shupe, 1979: 149-167).

All evidence on the New Religious Right, defined operationally as the Moral Majority, points in a sociologically recognizable, indeed familiar, direction. Earlier analyses of similar reactionary, politically motivated religious crusades, such as anti-pornography advocates (Zurcher *et al*, 1971) anti-Communists (Hofstadter, 1963), and Prohibitionists (Gusfield, 1963) strongly suggest that Falwell's Moral Majority represents one case of the religio-political phenomenon of "status politics". That is, we are witnessing organized attempts by persons to maintain (or guard against perceived threats to) their groups' self-defined status positions, where status is understood in the terms of German sociologist Max Weber as a cluster of prestige factors such as lifestyle goals and common belief loyalties.

There have been more recent studies of evangelicals involved in politics using a similar conceptual perspective: That of "lifestyle defense". Examples would be Page and Clelland's (1978) research on groups seeking to ban textbooks and Lorentzen's (1980) study of a campaign to elect evangelical politicians. In these studies the campaigns and crusades were interpreted as rearguard actions of

fundamentalist Christians who believe their ideal and/or actual moral worlds as crumbling in the wake of increasing
secularization and a humanistic morality that ranges from
liberal to irreligious. These Christians saw liberalism,
however exemplified in its religious/social/political/eco-
nomic forms, as bankrupt in its ability to deliver on its
promise of a safer, healthier, happier America. Once again,
such a perspective would conclude, we are seeing fundamentalist Christians reappearing after half a decade of igno-
miny following the repeal of Prohibition and the discrediting
"Scopes Trial" to reassert their biblically based morality
and dreams for American society. Only this time they have
been aided in delivering their message by the sophisticated
electronic church, with all its image-producing power. It
is, however, old wine in new bottles.

Yet simply mastering video technology is not the complete answer to how this fundamentalist resurgence has managed to create a myth of its own popular support that has
been accepted, at least temporarily, by many politicians
and journalists. There are at least two other key elements,
one of which has been the ability of leaders such as Jerry
Falwell to co-opt the publicity normally attached to single-
issue interest groups pressuring for anti-abortion, anti-
pornography, and even anti-evolution laws. By appearing
visibly and with much ballyhoo at rallies and conventions
(such as the 1981 National Affairs Briefing and Pro-Life
Rally, both staged in Dallas), by holding their own press
conferences simultaneously, and by repeating their claims
of broad popular support (with no immediate evidence to
the contrary) they have created the illusion that somehow
they represent and can thus speak for these various single-
issue groups. Pro-life and anti-pronography causes were
not created by Jerry Falwell, but his presence at such a
rally can lend it the color, or impression, of being a Moral

Majority event.

These appearances and endorsements by Falwell and others thus have created the myth of mass support for the Moral Majority and a false picture of ideological consensus within that part of the population that does support the movement. By co-opting the publicity of various single-issue groups, New Religious Right leaders have developed a stereotype of their supporters such that someone who supports a given position on an issue such as abortion can be assumed to fall in line automatically and support conservative positions on other issues such as the Equal Rights Amendment. As we have seen, this stereotype is unrealistic, because while there are many single-issue groups, there really is no consensually organized Moral Majority constituency of any size. There is nothing in a person's support for a constitutional amendment to prohibit abortion that logically suggests that the same person will also prefer creation theory (which almost all biologists, geologists, and astronomers have relegated to the shelf as nothing more than biblical allegory dressed up in the guise of crank science -- see Gardner, 1957) to evolutionary theory except among a narrow segment within the fundamentalist Christians category. Surveys are more likely to find in the general population "inconsistencies" such as a Roman Catholic female employed as a professor of palentology who is pro-Equal Rights Amendment but who is in little sympathy with the scientific merits of creation theory. Such so-called "inconsistencies" in fact abound in the general population, as we found in Texas and as Simpson (1981) found in a national sample of Americans.

A second key element has been the gradually building conservative shift in the voting public's mood since 1976 and the election of populist president Jimmy Carter. Carter's inability to control a number of domestic and

international problems, coupled with Ronald Reagan's flair
for conveying a posture of certainty and optimism, unquestionably led many Americans to opt for change. It was indeed a national mood preexisting independent of the New Religious Right. This conclusion has been succinctly stated
by the executive director of the Texas American Civil Liberties Union, John Duncan:

> People were not voting their ideology but their
> frustrations. I don't think the people voted
> for the religious nuts; they voted for their
> pocketbooks. The Republicans benefitted [sic]
> from an economic backlash against Carter (Col-
> lier, 1981).

The moral righteousness which made Carter an appealing
candidate in 1976 was also a positive factor for Reagan in
1980, and his deliberate wooing of evangelicals (whom no-
body had yet assessed well in terms of their size and political potential) lent the unmistakable impression after
the election that he was indebted heavily to evangelicals
and fundamentalists for his victory. New Religious Right
preachers such as Falwell and Robison appeared to have unusually commanding clout in politics, directly telephoning
or talking with White House staff, if not the President, over
issues such as Sandra O'Connor's nomination to the Supreme
Court.

We do not dispute the existence of a real conservative
mood dominating the United States during the 1980 presidential and congressional elections. However, our findings in
this study, taken as a whole, suggest that the New Religious
Right merely rode to Ronald Reagan's landslide victory on the
coattails of this more general mood and that conservative
voting patterns largely had little to do with theology or
morality. In short, Ronald Reagan would have been elected
whether or not the Moral Majority or the New Religious Right

had ever existed.

Social movements are by definition efforts directed
to achieving social change of institutions, challenging the
status quo. That is, they seek to accomplish that which
they perceive is necessary or desirable but is not yet at-
tained. Thus there is an irony in the fact that the flag-
ship organization of a movement made up of one of the smaller, more dogmatic religious minorities in American society
chose the label "Moral Majority, Inc." for its formal name.
The first two words suggest its aspirations as well as its
ability, however short-lived, to "pass" as a truly majority
voice of most Americans. The third word (actually the ab-
breviation for a corporation) suggests the sophistication
by which it has been able to accomplish this image-creation.
In terms of technology, evangelicals and fundamentalists
have undeniably come of age, if not of numbers.

However, the New Religious Right indisputably remains
a minority social movement, its goals yet unachieved and
its voice as yet unrepresented in the corridors of political
power. Its ultimate accomplishments cannot, of course, be
accurately forecast, but its small popular support base and
similarity to past moral crusades of sectarian Christians
indicate an eventual demise and submergence until, in the
reliably cyclical pattern of American Christianity, we are
once more visited with revival tempered by whatever current
issues and shaped by available technologies.

CHAPTER VIII

WHAT SHALL WE MAKE OF THE MORAL MAJORITY
AND THE NEW RELIGIOUS RIGHT?

What, indeed, are we as citizens to make of the Moral
Majority and the New Religious Right? Studies have demonstrated, both in our own Texas findings and in national
opinion polls, its factually low esteem among the general
population and among clergymen in particular. We have
shown the rather clear limitations of its support: fundamentalist (white) Christianity. We found no multi-racial,
interdenominational support base for the New Religious
Right even in the Bible-belt south. In fact, the movement's
supporters were the most likely to be anti-Semitic and anti-
Catholic of our respondents. These are not matters of arbi-
trary speculation or our personal opinions. Rather, they
are hard facts.

Yet on a daily basis policy makers and opinion-shapers
-- that is, legislators, and public officials, clergy, and
journalists -- are faced with decisions as to how to respond to the claims of Jerry Falwell and others. They must
decide, insofar as they have reliable information, how to
report, evaluate, or respond to the claims of leaders in
this conservative religio-political movement. It is to such

professionals that we direct our concluding remarks. While
such comments may appear partisan or politically motivated,
they are actually intended as guides for interpreting the
Moral Majority and the New Religious Right in light of ex-
isting research.

First, to legislators we reiterate the direction to
which *all* social science findings have pointed:

(1)   that the New Religious Right is no true
       "Majority" social movement;

(2)   that the conservative bent of many voters
       in the United States during the 1980 elec-
       tion was in no way initiated by or depen-
       dent upon fundamentalist-evangelical lead-
       ers such as Jerry Falwell or James Robi-
       son;

(3)   and that in fact as of 1981 the general
       voting public repudiated this movement
       twice as often as it endorsed it *when it
       had even heard of it.*

Politically speaking, though a relatively small bloc of organized voters could conceivably present the deciding edge
in a close election, the New Religious Right is not a force
to be reckoned with in most cases. It is true that conservative New Right groups such as the National Conservative
Political Action Committee have targeted certain "liberal"
politicians for defeat in elections, but in some cases (as
in our own state) they have not shown notable success and
in other cases it is far from clear that they played a de-
cisive role in influencing the electorate.

The conservative orientation that many Americans feel
towards Washington and the federal government is another
thing. It is real and helped Ronald Reagan attain the pres-
idency. However, the fundamentalist Christians in this
country cannot take credit either for creating or cultiva-

ting those sentiments among most Americans. Numerically speaking, they are simply too tiny a proportion of the citizenry. There is good reason to believe that in the 1980 elections most Americans voted more on the basis of economic than moralistic issues.

Second, we remind clergy of the significant differences of opinion among their colleagues on many social issues as well as on the idea of the religious institution becoming formally involved in politics. Neither we nor most ministers would advocate that they abrogate their position as moral leaders and ignore politics. However, the delicate distinction between taking a moralistic stance on a specific issue such as prayer in school or abortion and proclaiming *the* Christian position on that issue seems important to uphold, regardless of the effort. There can be room for honest theological disputes within and between denominations, just as there can be disagreement over social issues among citizens, without condemning one's opponents as heretical, un-Christian or un-American. As Dunn (1970) has shown in a readable little book entitled *Politics: A Guidebook for Christians,* clergypersons have an obligation both to their congregations as well as to the Constitution which safeguards their freedom of belief to monitor and exhort on social issues in a responsible way. To claim, as Jerry Falwell (among others) has done so often, that there is *one* Christian posture on a number of complex, sensitive issues simply creates the absurdity of many sincere, dedicated Christian clergy being condemned as un-Christian. No one man or movement can define for all time the domain of the Christian citizen's responsibilities.

Third, for journalists we have reserved a critical word. Journalists in the past have seized on the sensationalistic aspects of the New Religious Right and "milked" the topic for its drama. They have uncritically accepted

as fact whatever wild and unfounded numbers on membership
and support groups such as the Moral Majority have released. In fact, much of the illusion that the New Religious Right has either a substantial following or a significant political following (which much of the press and
politicians are coming to realize as an illusion) is the
by-product or artifact of shoddy investigation. It is still
not uncommon in our local Dallas-Fort Worth newspapers to
see the whole subject treated uncritically, journalists ac-
cepting at face value New Religious Right spokespersons'
claims of their own importance.

    We are aware, certainly, of the realistic editorial
and time pressures on individual reporters that make the
necessary background investigation difficult, but if jour-
nalism is more than merely repeating speculation, pipe-
dreams and exaggeration, then such preliminary work must be
done. There is now an adequate body of research, cited in
our bibliography and not inaccessible to journalists, to
provide such an empirical background.

    We believe that the three groups of professionals ad-
dressed above, as well as others, need to have a factual
basis for responding to the New Religious Right. Otherwise suspicion and ignorance may escalate the conflict between this movement and larger social institutions as time
goes on. It is that lack of understanding the New Religious
Right's true parameters, rather than any "isms" or pseudo-
struggle of Christians against non-Christians, that our research is intended to correct.

APPENDIX A

ADDITIONAL TABLES FOR CHAPTER SIX

TABLE 34: THE RELATIONSHIP BETWEEN DENOMINATION AND ATTI-
           TUDES TOWARD ABORTION AMONG THE CLERGY

ABORTION	FUNDAMENTAL		CONSERVATIVE		MODERATES		CATHOLICS	
	N	%	N	%	N	%	N	%
Agree	32	76	31	54	9	25	9	90
Disagree	10	24	26	46	27	75	1	10
Total	42	100.0	57	100.0	36	100.0	10	100.0

x^2 = 25.72   Pr. = .0000   V = .42

TABLE 35: THE RELATIONSHIP BETWEEN DENOMINATION AND ATTI-
           TUDES TOWARD E.R.A. AMONG THE CLERGY

E.R.A.	FUNDAMENTAL		CONSERVATIVE		MODERATES		CATHOLICS	
	N	%	N	%	N	%	N	%
Favor	20	48	24	44	30	86	6	67
Oppose	22	52	31	56	5	14	3	33
Total	42	100.0	55	100.0	35	100.0	9	100.0

x^2 = 17.6   Pr. = .0005   V = .35

TABLE 36: THE RELATIONSHIP BETWEEN DENOMINATION AND ATTI-
           TUDES TOWARD PRAYER IN SCHOOL AMONG THE CLERGY

PRAYER	FUNDAMENTAL		CONSERVATIVE		MODERATES		CATHOLICS	
	N	%	N	%	N	%	N	%
Favor	31	76	25	43	16	44	9	90
Oppose	10	24	33	57	20	56	1	10
Total	41	100.0	58	100.0	36	100.0	10	100.0

x^2 = 16.9   Pr. = .0007   V = .34

TABLE 37:   THE RELATIONSHIP BETWEEN DENOMINATION AND ATTI-
            TUDES TOWARD CREATION THEORY IN SCHOOL AMONG
            THE CLERGY

CREATION	FUNDAMENTAL		CONSERVATIVE		MODERATES		CATHOLICS	
	N	%	N	%	N	%	N	%
Favor	34	81	33	55	10	29	4	44
Oppose	8	19	27	45	25	71	5	56
Total	42	100.0	60	100.0	35	100.0	9	100.0

$x^2 = 21.7$ Pr. = .0001   V = .39

TABLE 38:   THE RELATIONSHIP BETWEEN DENOMINATION AND ATTI-
            TUDES TOWARD RIGHTS FOR HOMOSEXUALS AMONG THE
            CLERGY

HOMOSEXUALS	FUNDAMENTAL		CONSERVATIVE		MODERATES		CATHOLICS	
	N	%	N	%	N	%	N	%
Favor	2	5	15	25	19	56	5	50
Oppose	38	95	44	75	15	44	5	50
Total	40	100.0	59	100.0	34	100.0	10	100.0

$x^2 = 25.8$ Pr. = .0000   V = .42

TABLE 39:   THE RELATIONSHIP BETWEEN DENOMINATION AND ATTI-
            TUDES TOWARD PORNOGRAPHY AMONG THE CLERGY

PORNOGRAPHY	FUNDAMENTAL		CONSERVATIVE		MODERATES		CATHOLICS	
	N	%	N	%	N	%	N	%
Favor More Control	38	93	46	77	22	63	6	60
Do Not Favor More Control	3	7	14	23	13	37	4	40
Total	41	100.0	60	100.0	35	100.0	10	100.0

$x^2 = 11.18$ Pr. = .01   V = .28

BIBLIOGRAPHY

Adorno, T.W., *et al.*, *The Authoritarian Personality* (New York, 1950).

Armstrong, Ben, *The Electric Church* (Nashville, 1979).

Bakker, Jim and Robert Paul Lamb, *Move That Mountain!* (Plainfield, N.J., 1976).

Becker, Howard S., *Outsiders* (New York, 1966).

Bellah, Robert N., "Civil Religion in America" in *Religion in America* (Boston, 1968).

Briggs, Kenneth A., "TV Evangelism Dangerous, Graham Says" in *Fort Worth Star-Telegram* (1981).

Bromley, David G. and Anson D. Shupe, Jr., *Strange Gods: The Great American Cult Scare* (Boston, 1982).

_____, *"Moonies" in America: Cult, Church, and Crusade* (California, 1979).

Collier, Dick, "The Noisy Minority" in *Shorthorn* (Texas, 1981).

Cox, Harvey, *Turning East* (New York, 1977).

Dallas Times Herald, "Over 600,000 Quit Viewing Gospel Shows" (1981a).

_____, "Moral Majority Funds Double, Audit Revealed" (1981b).

Dunn, James M., (ed.) *Politics: A Guidebook for Christians* (Texas, 1970).

Falwell, Jerry, "My Turn: The Maligned Moral Majority in *Newsweek* (1981a).

_____, Interview with Rev. Jerry Falwell (Texas, 1981b).

_____, "The Silent Pulpits of America" (Virginia, 1981c).

Fort Worth Star-Telegram, "Electronic Church Leads Its
    Flocks to the Airwaves" (1980).

Gallup, George, "The Gallup Poll -- Attitudes Toward the
    Moral Majority Explored in Survey" (1980).

Gardner, Martin, *Fads and Fallacies in the Name of Science*
    (New York, 1957).

Grandmeyer, G.A. and R.S. Denisoff, "Status Politics: An
    Appraisal of the Application of A Concept" in *Pacific
    Sociological Review* (1963).

Greene, Johnny, "The Astonishing Wrongs of the New Moral
    Right" in *Playboy* (1981).

Gusfield, Joseph R., *Symbolic Crusade: Status Politics and
    the American Temperence Movement* (Urbana, 1963).

Gwynne, Peter, "'Scopes II' in California" in *Newsweek*
    (1981).

Hadden, Jeffrey K. and Charles K. Swann, *Prime Time Preach-
    ers: The Rising Power of Televangelism* (Massachu-
    setts, 1981).

Harrell, Jr., David Edwin., "The Roots of the Moral Major-
    ity: Fundamentalism Revisited" (Minnesota, 1981).

_____, *All Things Are Possible: The
    Healing and Charismatic Revivals in Modern America*
    (Bloomington, 1975).

Harris, Louis, "Harris Survey: Moral Majority Shouldn't
    Control TV" in *Fort Worth Star-Telegram* (1981).

Haught, James A., "The God Biz" in *Penthouse* (1980).

Hofstadter, Richard, "The Pseudo-Conservative Revolt" in
    *The Radical Right: The New American Right Expanded
    and Updated* (New York, 1963).

Johnson, Merle A., *How To Be Happy in the Non-Electric
    Church* (Nashville, 1977).

Johnson, Stephen D. and Joseph B. Tamney., "The Christian
    Right and the 1980 Presidential Election" (1980).

Jones, Jim, "Their Cups Runneth Dry: TV Evangelists Sound
    Financial Crisis Alarm" in *Fort Worth Star-Telegram*
    (1981).

Jorstad, Erling, *Evangelicals in the White House: The Cultural Maturation of Born Again Christianity 1960-1980* (New York, 1981).

Kelley, Dean M., *Why Conservative Churches Are Growing* (New York, 1972).

Lester, Barbara J. and A. Paul Romjue, "Correlates of Conservatism: A Consideration of the Electronic Church" (Toronto, 1981).

Lipset, Seymour Martin, *Revolution and Counter-revolution* (New York, 1970).

_____ and Earl Raab, "The Election and the Evangelicals" in *Commentary* (1981).

Lorentzen, Louise J., "Evangelical Life Style Concerns Expressed in Political Action" in *Sociological Analysis* (1980).

Lovelace, John, "Panel to Study TV Station PUrchase" in *The Texas Methodist* (1981).

Mariani, John, "Television Evangelism: Milking the Flock" in *Saturday Review* (1979).

Martin, William, "The Birth of a Media Myth" in *The Atlantic* (1981a).

_____, "God's Angry Man" in *Texas Monthly* (1981b).

_____, "Heavenly Hosts" in *Texas MOnthly* (1979).

Marty, Martin E., *Righteous Empire: The Protestant Experience in America* (New York, 1970)

Neuhaus, Cable, "Praise the Lord on TV -- the "700 Club" in *The Humanist* (1978).

Newsweek, "Jerry Falwell's Vanishing Clout" (1981).

Page, Ann L. and Donald A. Clelland, "The Kanawha County Textbook Controversy: A Study of the Politics of Life Style Concern" in *Social Forces* (1978).

Parmley, Helen and Sam Attlesey, "New Right Crusade Loses Steam" in *Dallas Morning News* (1981).

Peterson, Bill and Barry Sussman, "Moral Majority Is Growing in Recognition, But It Remains Unknown to Half the Public" in *The Washington Post* (1981).

Quebedeaux, Richard, *The Worldly Evangelicals* (New York, 1980).

_____, *The New Charismatics* (New York, 1976).

Robbins, Thomas and Dick Anthony, *In Gods We Trust: New Patterns of Religious Pluralism in America* (New Jersey, 1981).

Sandeen, Ernest R., "Fundamentalism and American Identity" in *The Social Meanings of Religion* (Chicago, 1974).

Sasthi, Brata and Andrew Duncan, "Penthouse Interview: Reverend Jerry Falwell" in *Penthouse* (1981).

Shupe, Jr., Anson D. and William A. Stacey, "The Moral Majority Constituency" in *The New Christian Right: Mobilization and Legitimization* (1982).

Shupe, Jr., Anson D. and James R. Wood, "Sources of Leadership Ideology in Dissident Clergy" in *Sociological Analysis* (1973).

Simpson, John H., "Support for the Moral Majority and Status Politics in Contemporary America" (Toronto, 1981).

Solod, Lisa, "The Nutshell Interview: Jerry Falwell" in *Nutshell* (1981/82).

Suplee, Curt, "The Power and the Glory in the New Senate" in *The Washington Post* (1981).

Valentine, Foy, "How to Preach on Political Issues" in *Politics: A Guidebook for Christians* (Texas, 1970).

Wallace, Anthony, *Religion: An Anthropological View* (New York, 1966).

_____, "Revitalization Movements" in *American Anthropologist* (1956).

Waters, Harry F., The New Right TV Hits List" in *Newsweek* (1981).

Weidel, Arthur and L.J. Davis, "Praise the Lord and Pass the Contributions" in *Penthouse* (1982).

Weissmann, Arnie, "Building The Tower of Babel" in *Texas Outlook* (1981   ).

Wilson Bryan, *The Social Impact of New Religious Movements* (New York, 1981).

Wimberley, Ronald C., "Continuity in the Measurement of Civil Religion" in *Sociological Analysis* (1979).

_____, "Testing the Civil Religion Hypothe-sis" in *Sociological Analysis* (1976).

_____, "The Civil Religious Dimension: Is It There?" in *Social Forces* (1976).

Zurcher, Jr., Louis, "The Anti-Pornography Campaign: A Symbolic Crusade" in *Social Problems* (1971).

INDEX

Abortion, Attitudes on, 34-36,
    67-70; Clergy attitudes
    towards, 78-82,89
Angley, Ernest, 62
Anti-Catholicism Scale, 22-23
Anti-Semitism Scale, 22-23
Armstrong, James, 76
Bakker, Jim, 62
Baptist Joint Committee on
    public affairs, 94
Billings, Robert, 2
Bush, George, 6
Carter, Jimmy, 3,99-100
Christian Broadcasting Net-
    work, 54
Christian Orthodoxy, see Re-
    ligious Orthodoxy, 21-22
Christian Women's National
    Concerns, 41
Church Religiosity Scale, 22
    and Support for Moral Ma-
    jority, 52-53; Minority
    Responses to, 70-71
Civil Religion Scale, 20-21,
    39,48-49,51,58-63; Minority
    Responses to, 70-71
Clements, Bill, 66
Clergy, Opinions about Moral
    Majority, 75-92; Survey of
    24-25
Conservative Caucus, 1
Copeland, Kenneth, 62
Creation theory, Attitudes
    towards, 35, 38-39, 67-70;
    Clergy Attitudes towards,
    78-80, 85-86, 89
Dallas Pro-Life Rally, 5,14,98
Darwinian Evolution, 31,35,38-39
    67-70; Clergy attitudes to-
    wards, 78-80
Davis, Cullen T., 14,41
Dixon, Craig, 75
Duncan, John, 100
Dunn, James, 94, 105
Electronic Church, 7-8,11,24;
    As a Southern phenomenon,15;
    Methodist General Confer-
    ence, 55; National Council

of Churches of Christ
    55-56; See also Media
    Religiosity; United
    States Catholic Con-
    ference, 55-56; Uni-
    ted Presbyterian
    Church in USA, 55
Equal Rights Amendment,
    1,14,24,67-70; Atti-
    tudes towards, 35-37;
    Clergy attitudes to-
    wards, 78-83,89,99
Falwell, Jerry, 1,2,4,5,
    6,7,8,9,11,14,16,24,
    36,40,41,47,48,54,56,
    57,62,75,76,93,96,98
Graham, Billy, 62
Homosexuals, equal
    rights for, 78-80,87-
    89
Humbard, Rex, 62
James Robison Evangelis-
    tic Association,14
Media Religiosity Scale,
    22,58-63; and support
    for Moral Majority,
    54-57; Media respon-
    ses to, 70-71
Moral Majority, As ex-
    amples of status
    politics, 97; general
    awareness of, 30,31,
    94; Minority support
    for, 65-74; Origins,
    16; Relation to elec-
    tronic church, 3;
    Relation to Fundamen-
    tal resurgence, 2-4;
    Religious background
    of supporters, 40-41;
    Religious prejudice
    and support, 41-44
National Affairs Brief-
    ing, 14,98
National Conservative
    Political Action Com-
    mittee, 1,104

New Religious Right, indications of popular support for, 4-6; indications of lack of popular support, 6-9; see Moral Majority

Nixon, Richard, 62

O'Connor, Sandra, 1,100

Phyllis, Howard, 14

Pornography, legislation to control 78-80, 87-87, 89

Prayer in school, attitudes towards, 35,38,67-70; clergy attitudes towards, 78-84, 89

Reagan, Ronald, 1,2,4,6,7,14, 100

Religious Orthodoxy Scale, 21,58-63,70-71; and support for Moral Majority, 53-54

Religious Roundtable, 1,14,24, 41

Roberts, Oral, 7,56,62

Robertson, Pat, 7,55,62

Robison, James, 1,5,8,11,13,14, 16,24,41,47,54,57,62,77,93

Roman Catholics, see Moral Majority religious background of supporters

Schlafley, Phyllis, 5,14,36

Schuller, Robert, 56, 62

Scope's "Monkey trial", 2

Secular humanism, 31-34,38-39, 79

Sex education, attitudes towards, 35,67-70

Swaggart, Jimmy, 62

Texas American Civil Liberties Union, 100

Unification Church of America, 97

Washington For Jesus Rally, 5

Weber, Max, 97

Weyrich, Paul, 14

Wildmon, Donald E., 93

STUDIES IN AMERICAN RELIGION

I. Suzanne Geissler, **Jonathan Edwards to Aaron Burr, Jr: From the Great Awakening to Democratic Politics**
II. Ervin Smith, **The Ethics of Martin Luther King, Jr.**
III. Nancy Manspeaker, **Jonathan Edwards: Bibliographical Synopses**
IV. Erling Jorstad, **Evangelicals in the White House: The Cultural Maturation of Born Again Christianity, 1960-1981**
V. Anson Shupe & William A. Stacey, **Born Again Politics and the Moral Majority: What Social Surveys Really Show**

FOR A COMPLETE LIST OF TITLES AND PRICES PLEASE WRITE:
The Edwin Mellen Press
P.O. Box 450
Lewiston, New York 14092